THIS TIME OF SALVATION

THIS TIME OF SALVATION

Bernard Häring

Translated by
Arlene Swidler

HERDER AND HERDER

1966
HERDER AND HERDER NEW YORK
232 Madison Avenue, New York 10016

Original edition:
Die Gegenwärtige Heilsstunde, first half,
Erich Wewel Verlag, Freiburg im Breisgau, 1964.

Imprimi potest:	William Coudreau, C.SS.R.
	Superior General
Nihil obstat:	Thomas J. Beary
	Censor Librorum
Imprimatur:	✠Robert F. Joyce
	Bishop of Burlington
	February 23, 1966

Library of Congress Catalog Card Number: 66-16947
© 1966 by Herder and Herder, Incorporated
Manufactured in the United States

CONTENTS

5

CONTENTS

6

THIS TIME OF SALVATION

TIME OF LOVE

The Forgotten Brotherhood

MAY we use the daring expression, "The Church *is* love"? Only of God is it essentially and unrestrictedly true—"he *is* love." He alone is good. Love is his innate life. Of himself he possesses love; in it he fulfills the triune abundance of his being.

Love is the essence of the Church, though not a love which she possesses of herself; she is love as the bride beloved by the Lord, as the one endowed to overflowing measure by divine love, the one called by love,[1] called together to love, but one whose abundance of love is always dependent on the human readiness to respond to love. In this world the Church must be the living, accessible witness of the fact that God is love and truly wishes co-celebrants of his love in a single great community of all who love. The Church lives in the fellowship of love, which is the gift of purest love. It is her vocation to make this fellowship of love existential for man.

THE COLLEGIALITY OF THE BISHOPS

Anyone who tries to understand the Church primarily as an organization, as an external force of order, and only secondarily

[1] Perhaps the word *"ecclesia,"* ἐκκλησία > ἐκ-καλέω, can also be understood in this sense.

11

as a fellowship of love, misunderstands the purpose of ecclesiastical power of order and the entire Church from the ground up; for hierarchy means the holy order of love, intended to serve love (*diakonia*), to defend the witness of love from disintegration and from every inner opposition. The more the Church is love, the greater is her authority, the more credible is her proclamation of faith, the more true and pleasing to God is her worship.

This can be heard with unavoidable clarity in, among other places, the prayer of Jesus as high priest: "Holy Father, keep them in thy name which thou hast given me, that they may be one, even as we are one" (Jn. 17, 11). Father and Son are one in the love of the Holy Spirit. They are one being. The community of disciples—the apostles, primarily—is to be an image of the wondrous unity in love between the Father and the Son. Indeed, the goal of the new covenant, which the apostolic office and the priesthood also serve, is to tear down every wall of separation by sin and to call everyone back into the blessed unity of the love of God.

"And for their sake I consecrate myself, that they also may be consecrated in truth" (Jn. 17, 19). The incarnate Son of the Father *consecrates himself for us*; he dedicates himself vicariously for us in an incomprehensible loving solidarity, as an offering by which we too may be so consecrated in truth. But that means that those consecrated in truth must make themselves the servants of all in the manner of Christ, must consecrate themselves in an unsurpassable solidarity with men; in other words, they must sacrifice themselves. Like Christ, they must bear death in their body in order to realize the unity of love.

From the construction of the high-priestly prayer it is clear that brotherhood must first be apparent in those especially summoned, in the bishops; their unity among themselves according to the image of the Trinity, their consecration (their readiness

12

for service and sacrifice) according to the model of the sacrificial lamb which takes away the sin of the world, is the core of Christian brotherhood.

The collegiality of the bishops, which is one of the fundamental teachings of the Second Vatican Council, must above all be seen in light of the mystery of unity and love. The prayer of the Lord in the room of the last supper after the institution of the eucharist and the sacrament of ordination, which is fulfilled in the apostles and their successors, explains the meaning, the gift, and the commission of the sacrament. No one who thinks primarily of juridical power over others or even understands (we should say misunderstands) the composition of the Church as primarily power and force, will be able to comprehend the teaching of collegiality. It deals primarily and basically with a *sacramental reality*. Just as the Church as a whole is the sacrament of the love of God in Christ Jesus, so too the apostles (bishops), and the priests of the entire Church gathered around them, make visible and existential the mystery of love which calls them together in consecration. The collegiality of the bishops signifies a *sacramental reality*: the sacrament of solidarity. From this moral obligations flow first of all. But because the juridical aspect must not stand apart as foreign to the sacramental and moral order, collegiality, which corresponds to the needs of the time, should also make itself effectual in the juridical and administrative structures. That does not mean letting juridicism and the struggle for power in through a back door, but the ordering of the juridical and spiritual power as a visible sign of a sacramental reality under the primacy of love.

The visibility of the Church does not primarily mean—as Cardinal Ernesto Ruffini of Palermo suggested in the council chamber in rejecting the biblical expression *"mysterium"*—a complex of juridical forces and structures. The word *"mysterium-sacrament"* means a "visible sign" of a reality not naturally belonging to or accessible to man. The Church is the sacrament of love. Everything about her and in her must breathe such a love, solidarity, collegiality, fatherliness, and brotherliness that it points visibly to the concealed reality that comes from God. From this it is evident that the teaching of the collegiality of the bishops does not mean a theology of their power as opposed to the power of the Roman Curia, but a theology of brotherhood,[2] which places the fatherhood of the pope as their head, their own fatherhood to the faithful, and the brotherhood of all the faithful to one another in the foreground of consideration.

Office in the Church, *diakonia*, means community and solidarity of love, but also common service to all, the common creation of brotherhood. But the price which must be paid unceasingly for this is like the price of Christ: "Greater love has no man than this, that a man lay down his life for his friends" (Jn. 15, 13). The day-by-day dying of the old man, the rejection of the egotistical way of thinking, is always the presupposition of unity within the innermost circle of the community of brothers and the beginning of the return home of the many in love.

BROTHERHOOD OF THE FAITHFUL AS REFLECTION OF COLLEGIALITY

The Lord then continues in his prayer: "I do not pray for these only, but also for those who are to believe in me through their word, that they may all be one; even as thou, Father, art in me, and I in thee, that they also may be in us, so that the world may believe that thou hast sent me" (Jn. 17, 20f.). The basic presupposition for this, the fact that the gospel comprehends constantly larger circles—from the love of the triune God, from him sent by the love of the Father, and from the sending of the Holy Spirit (ultimately always the gospel of the mystery of the tri-unity)—is the presentation of the brotherly unity not only

[2] See the *Constitution on the Church*, Chapter III, Articles 22, 23, 28.

14

of the apostles but also of all those who have come to faith through their words and the example of their love.

Again the high-priestly prayer takes up the same earnest plea, this time in the perspective of the δόξα, the glory of love shared by the Son and the Father for all eternity, shining for us in the incarnate Son, particularly in the Easter mystery of his resignation and his exaltation accomplished through his resignation. "The glory which thou hast given me I have given to them, that they may be one even as we are one, I in them and thou in me, that they may become perfectly one, so that the world may know that thou hast sent me and hast loved them even as thou hast loved me. . . . I made known to them thy name, and I will make it known, that the love with which thou hast loved me may be in them, and I in them" (Jn. 17, 22-26). The primary and most eminent goal of the manifestation of God's glory of love, of the outward forms of salvation, and of the grace acting within us is the brotherly unity through which we glorify God worthily, through which, as it were, we are the glory of God on earth. In this way God wishes to convince the rest of men of the saving power of his glorious love, that they too, unanimously unified in one faith and one love, may give honor to him and experience the enrapturing power of his glory.

All the bridal gifts of the covenant are gifts from the heart of the triune God. Thus from their innermost being they urge us to manifest the love of God through the unity of those who are so beloved. The revelation of God's name as Father by the Son, whom the Father has consecrated as a sacrifice for us, obliges us, the family of God, in a special way to be witness to the love of Christ acting in us to create unity. This is true not only of the love between individuals, but especially of the manifestation of the unity of the Christian *community* of love. The most exalted, most glowing prayer and the most intimate admonishment of the Lord in the chamber of the last supper lead us into the inner holiness and mystery of the redemption which we celebrate in the eucharist. The eucharistic celebration should form us ever more intimately into a community of love.

What we have briefly indicated here in this single excerpt from holy Scripture can and must be still more deeply confirmed and interpreted by the theology of the covenant, which teaches us that we can partake of the love of God only in the measure as we live in the covenant of love, in the community of love of the people of the covenant, and thus bear witness to that love with which God has concluded the new covenant.

Furthermore, *sacramental theology* must creatively work with the treasures of holy Scripture and tradition and thereby reveal the sacramental power which testifies to and establishes community, and its essential commission to brotherhood, to solidarity in the community. According to classical theology, it is first of all baptism, penance, and the eucharist which are to designate and bring about the unity and brotherhood of the people of God. Of them it is especially valid to say: "*Res et sacramentum est unitas populi fidelium.*"

The wonderful constitution of the Second Vatican Council on the holy liturgy not only stresses emphatically the teaching that the eucharist is a sign of unity, a bond of charity,[3] and that the liturgy "moves the faithful . . . to be 'one in holiness'"; the entire work of renewal also strives practically that by the celebration itself the faithful will with understanding and feeling be incited to love, will be educated to brotherhood.

It is a very pleasant task for the dogmaticians to demonstrate that the Church is the great sign of divine love and the community of those handing on the love of God.[4] It is very easy to

[3] The *Constitution on the Sacred Liturgy*, Chapter II, Article 47; Chapter I, Article 10.

[4] For the positive view of the Church as brotherliness, see J. Ratzinger, "Christliche Brüderlichkeit," in *Der Seelsorger* XXVIII, 1957–1958, pp. 387–429; H. Schürmann, "Gemeinde als Bruderschaft," in *Ite missa est*, Paderborn, 1958, pp. 5–19; B. Häring, "The Significance of the Sacraments," in this volume.

show that the sacraments as Christ intended them are in their innermost being acting signs of unity, speaking signs of the brotherhood in the family of God. That is very easy to demonstrate, of course, if one stays within the scope of mere doctrine. But the questions immediately become disturbing, burning, disquieting, and accusing when we examine our consciences to see whether we, the "we" which ought to embody the brotherhood of the Church, actually make the good news of the triune love of God experienceable and credible to the world.

THE FORGOTTEN BROTHERHOOD

The more we consider the ideal—the true, real, and serious intent of Christ and the gracious possibility of complete unity and brotherhood imparted and declared to us in the sacraments —the more we are accused by the reality: lacerated Christendom, the egotism of the individual and very especially group-egotism, the accumulated sins of hateful or disdainful speech not only towards the Christians separated by ecclesiastical doctrine and unity—and that is grave enough—but even towards other groups and members within the one holy Church. Certainly, in world congresses (in the Eucharistic World Congress, the World Congress of the Lay Apostolate) one rejoices that we do all belong to the same large family and that the flame of love is not yet quenched. But even there disharmony is seldom completely absent.

Does not the nationalism (even in some ecclesiastical circles) of the self-styled Christian peoples of Europe during the past hundred years accuse us all? The love of Christians was and is apparently not so great that it would tear down the wall of separation between "Greeks and Jews, slaves and free." And yet the apostle says that in Christ—that means, when we really live in conformity to the Christian way of life—such distinctions can no longer play a divisive role. Does the universal solidarity of the single Church really prevail, so that national groups exchange their talents and powers with one another even beyond the borders of race and nationality? Alongside one diocese with a superfluity of priests stand others with abandoned parishes. The lack of priests of one continent does not touch the heart of the richly blessed Christians of other lands. Here and there are bishops or vicars general who still use their powers to hinder any of those in their charge from going to the foreign missions. In the face of this lack of solidarity in Church life one should not be surprised that Christianity has not demonstrated the strength to withstand nationalism. Does one not hear even among "pious" Christians thoughtless, derogatory, unfair generalized judgments on other peoples?

Added to this is the wall of separation between the social classes. We Christians of the West did not have that strength of brotherhood which could have spared us the century of class hatred and the revolution of Communism. It is still hard even for us priests to enter into the spirit of real brotherhood in the manner of the worker.

The disease is so deep-seated that even in theological textbooks on dogma and morals, which ought to present principally the wonderful reality of love and the commandment of love, of brotherhood—yes, even in ascetics, in the teaching of perfection—the categories of individualism were allowed to spread. A purely imperative morality, inspired by positivism, is the most pointed expression of the gradual extinguishing of brotherhood and genuine sympathy. The apologetics of the past centuries believed it could convince the world with mere reasoned arguments that the Father sent us his Son. In sacramental theology, for example, dogmatics lost itself in long arguments over a physical or merely moral effectiveness of the sacraments. In doing this, the categories of Christian personalism and saving solidarity, by which the Christian sacraments are actually set worlds apart from all heathen rites, remained amazingly underdeveloped. But even now we still have not mentioned the deepest wounds. We mean the formalistic, individualistic distortion of the actual celebration of the sacraments, which are indeed essentially the signs of the covenant, of the unity of the new people of God in the covenant of love.

THE REDISCOVERY OF BROTHERHOOD IN THE CELEBRATION OF THE SACRAMENTS

Baptism is the feast of the family of God, which is given a new brother, a new sister. In its love the community of the faithful hands on to him the authentic witness of truth. This symbol of faith in the triune God and in Christ's work of salvation must shine upon this baptized soul in the unity of God's people. The community takes upon itself the responsibility for that spirit of harmony and love, for that atmosphere in the milieu in which the one reborn as a child of God can grow. To grow, however, can mean nothing else than to come to perfect love and unity.

But what actually have our administrations of baptism been like, the predominating baptisms in the maternity wards, baptisms performed "off in a corner"?—one resists using the correct term "baptismal celebration" here. Do they speak understandably and intelligibly to every man of that which is indeed *"res et sacramentum,"* the essential grace and the essential message of baptism? Do our Christians really experience again and again through the co-celebration of baptism that they are all one in Christ and can work out their salvation only in mutual love and responsibility, in unity?

In instruction for confirmation and the administration of that sacrament can we always see the apostolic teaching that all spiritual graces are given for the sake of the community, for the sake of the fulfillment of the mystical body of Christ? (St. Thomas explains the meaning of the sacramental symbol: As the balsam gushes forth and imparts its exquisite odor to all

19

about it, so the confirmed must above all be aware that his perfection exists in his care for the salvation of his neighbor, in unity and in love with his neighbor.)

The eminently social essential significance of the sacrament of penance finds forceful expression in the solemn rite which is still to be found today in the *Pontificale Romanum*. But in the actual manner in which faithful often receive the sacrament and the priests "administer" it, very many are no longer aware of the real and essential symbolic language of the sacrament: that reconciliation with God is possible and effective only through reconciliation with the community, in a return to brotherly unity and solidarity. In some confessional guides the love of neighbor is still hidden somewhere behind the fifth commandment, and even there is often referred to only in the relation of individual to individual. The Church community is only somewhat more perceptible in the demand that one fulfill the law of complete confession and in the authoritative majestic words of absolution. The idea of amendment is not widely understood for what it really is: a new relation of a child to God through a new spirit of brotherhood, a new relationship to the *familia Dei*.

In most parishes the celebration of the mystery of unity and brotherhood, the eucharist, stifles any thoughts of the truth so central to this sacrament, the truth that God is glorified primarily by the perfect unity and community of his children, in the loving unity of the Church, in the unity in the Holy Ghost. There have been constructed somewhat ephemeral images of a "pure cult" in which certain spirits seem the more exalted the less that the thought of their neighbor or the perceptible care for the community of love interferes. There are still many priests, the *Constitution on the Sacred Liturgy* and the many liturgical directives of the Holy Office notwithstanding, who are quite determined to continue to murmur the Mass for themselves; for if the priest must proclaim the gospel to the people audibly and must speak the prayers so that the people understand them and

20

can confirm them by an *Amen,* his piety, completely absorbed in itself, would be disturbed. It ought not only to be disturbed, but completely destroyed! For it is not the piety of Christ which in one and the same sacrifice turned completely to the Father in heaven and at the same time completely to fellow humans in need of redemption, to his bride, the holy Church. Christian piety distinguished itself from the Stoic ethic and from the Buddhist way of salvation not least by the deep feeling of the substantial unison of the praying Christian with the community, by the clear knowledge that one can have a completely personal relation to God only if one lives and prays in the covenant of love with the brothers and sisters.

One must nevertheless consider how enormously difficult it is for a Christian formed in the spirit of individualism, or for a priest with a sincerely pious attitude, to change suddenly now to an explicitly community-oriented form of worship. The change will not succeed at all if the soul is not at the same time engrossed by an entirely new attitude, a complete openness to the "family of God."

Precisely on this point we see that, existentially, the liturgy is absolutely the first source and school of brotherhood, but that nevertheless psychologically it does not become active and cannot develop its full community-establishing character if the care for brotherhood does not also occupy the principal place in parish life and in the total formation of Christian life. But on the other side an earnest sermon on brotherhood, on consummate love in unity, cannot in the long run seem credible if the actual manner of celebrating this great mystery of brotherly unity (the holy eucharist) forcefully contradicts this gracious truth and its specific commission.

"Sacramenta efficiunt quod figurant"[5] *et significant, quod efficiunt* (the sacraments effect what they signify and signify what they effect). From these meaningful perceptions, artic-

[5] *Summa theol.* III, q. 62, a. 1, ad 1.

ulated in the scholastic formulation, we can infer: *Sacramenta efficiunt unitatem, si eam significant* (the sacraments effect unity *insofar* as they signify this unity). The man who denies the sacraments their clearly experienceable character of community robs them of their specific efficacy. He does not awaken but destroys the disposition necessary for sacramental grace, which fosters community. Because this concerns the *sacramenta novae legis* (sacraments of the new law), we must add: the sacraments will bring forth the principal fruit of unity only if on the one hand we fully bring to realization the symbolism signifying their real unity, and on the other hand also admit the grace given in the sacrament as the real law of our life. Thus is brotherly community and harmony at the same time both the fruit of the eucharistic celebration and a preparation for the disposition necessary for a constantly fruitful celebration.

THE CONVERSION TO BROTHERHOOD IN PASTORAL CARE

The decisive source of power, which can confer on us the grace of the Christian sense of family in overflowing measure, is without doubt a sincere liturgy. What was for a long time an almost ineffective and incomprehensible symbol must again become an articulate, effective, and binding sign of the gathering love of God and the community of God assembled as a family, and of course in such a way that everyone is able to understand and participate in its accomplishment. There is without doubt much to say about this. We wish, however, to describe briefly a few symptomatic points which should indicate the way to a pastoral theology growing out of the spirit of communal liturgy.

The first thing we wish to name is the visible, perceptible unity and friendship of priests. It would certainly be beautiful and inspiring if the essential unity of the priesthood which exists among priests and between them and their bishop were perceptibly expressed, for example, in their conferences (and especially in eucharistic congresses and in priests' retreats) in a real and true *concelebratio.*[6] But the inner unison demanded by the sacrament in our intentions and thus in our prayers and actions and in our entire pastoral care must always and unfailingly become a visible reality.

If only the vertical union with the chancery holds us priests together, often not much remains besides an irritating organization; but if there also exists a strong horizontal bond in genuine priestly community and priestly friendship (not only between two, for genuine priestly friendship always leads to a greater love of the community), the relationship to ecclesiastical authority also becomes more interior and effective; and the prerequisites are thus created so that the common struggle and prayer will lead to knowledge of the *kairós* and to the accomplishment of its task. What has been said can be understood as analogous to the collegiality of the bishops with the pope as head. The office of Peter's successor comes to fruition completely only if horizontal unions of many members within the episcopacy also serve unity.

The growing acceptance of the missions preached to the people of whole areas, which are at bottom nothing but attempts to assist in the pastoral care of those areas, should be a widely visible encouragement for the brotherly cooperation of all pastors. The fruit of our pastoral care would be much richer if the people experienced our harmony in everything. Let us take as examples the vital efforts for a liturgy near to the people, which accents the community, or for the properly timed preparation of children for first communion by their parents. If only one pastor begins to turn his special attention to these great concerns while most of the neighboring pastors wait in the meantime benevolently or skeptically, one perhaps raising his eyebrows if the faithful come to speak to him of the matter, another scoffing

[6] The *Constitution on the Sacred Liturgy,* Chapter II, Article 57, grants even further latitude in these matters.

or criticizing strongly—will the people not necessarily be confused? If the blessing of unity is lacking, often even the best efforts will be a cause of great spiritual misfortune. A decisive breakthrough of a pastoral theology with a new orientation will succeed only if the priests of the same area are agreed with one another on it and in brotherly undertaking consider in common the ways and means best fitted for the special needs and possibilities in their district. The pastoral sociology of today makes clear the solidarity of the moral and religious condition of sociologically coherent areas on the basis of the involvement in the totality of the events of life. It can produce the elements for a common plan of action which more or less answers the actual exigencies of the hour. But ultimately all this has meaning and value only if it is begun and completed in the spirit of brotherhood and contributes to a constant deepening of the brotherly spirit. In this, obviously, everyone must at the proper time give up some of his favorite ideas; here and there he must give way. Finally, we must understand in this task that only through our assimilation to the death of Christ will the separating wall of dismemberment and disunity be demolished and remain demolished. The price of the necessary witness to unity must daily be paid anew by everyone.

From the experience of several years we can say that joint retreats of the clergy of a geographical area, centering on pastoral duties, obviously have the blessing of God in a special manner. They have greater power of penetration than if each priest made a retreat alone somewhere. The priests who must be united with one another in pastoral action should from time to time—for example, before a regional mission for the people— experience their unity in common prayer and in common listening to the word of God, in common searching for the will of God.

The cooperation of the priests of the various orders and congregations and the harmonious adjustment of their efforts to the needs of day-to-day pastoral care is a meaningful witness of brotherly unity.

We would next like to mention the unity between priests and lay apostles, a unity which on the one hand finds its principal central source and at the same time its form of expression in a celebration of the eucharistic sacrifice and sacraments which is directed more towards the people and what is characteristic of them, but which must then also be realized in all questions of pastoral care. That obviously demands of both sides—of priests and of laity—a great gift of sympathy, patience, and a constant mystical death of egotism and of the rigid holding fast to traditional forms. Clericalism is a wall of separation which has in principle been torn down by the death of Christ, but which nevertheless again and again tries to rise out of the ashes. And the laity need much patience with us, for we have a long way to go to understand the world of today and, wherever it is necessary, to put aside everything which does not come from the gospel but has merely become a time-conditioned form and mentality of our profession. Only when we understand that the laity must also have patience with us will we likewise bring forth that patience which reconciles instead of offends. Once, in a college in which white, black, and yellow priests lived together, we heard a white complain, "One does need an immense patience with these Negroes; their cultural background is simply wretched." Later we had occasion to hear that the Negro and Oriental priests had immense patience with that white priest, a patience far greater and more admirable, when he in his intense "show of patience" betrayed his arrogance. He was completely unaware of his own narrow way of thinking. Only the spirit of brotherhood, sincere sympathy, and identifying love helps us to be one with our Christians and especially with our lay apostles.

One last thing to be named in this context is the apostolate to the milieu. The real key to the understanding of this is the mystery of the *"philadelphia,"* the incarnation of the supernatural

25

brotherhood in the very place where the natural communities stand and natural solidarity is at work.

The apostolate to the neighborhood does not attempt to delegate messengers of the pastor for the various neighborhood units; its goal is primarily to form community-establishing Christians. The solidarity of Christians must incarnate itself in the natural community, in the neighborhood, in one's work.

The apostolate to the milieu, so understood, reveals an analogy to the sacrament of marriage: this sacrament informs the natural loving community of the family and makes of this community in which the natural solidarity is strongest an image of the saving covenant between Christ and the Church. Not only married love but the entire life of the family community becomes through the sacrament a common way of salvation in solidarity. From the smallest cell of the Church, the family, this law must, analogically, communicate itself to every natural community. The two most important communities for this seem to us to be the neighborhood and working life. For this reason we stress these two forms of the apostolate in our mission to the people today. The visible and perceptible realization of Christian brotherhood in the neighborhood, in work, or in the professional group can also revitalize the life of organizations, which to some extent has become sluggish, and unite it organically with the pastoral care in the entire community.

In this context we must also mention groups of families which struggle in common for the realization of their family ideals and work in common to bring about better thinking and talking on marriage and the family in their surroundings.

The embodiment of Christian fraternal feeling in the individual milieu or circles of life is of special significance as a result of our often all too large parishes. In many cases they can be divided only with difficulty; but they can and must in all cases be organized into a whole variety of subgroups.

The Church of God must be visibly present in each family, in each neighborhood, in each milieu, but also in the entire parish as the community of love and peace, of unity and co-responsibility. From holy Scripture we learn that every local community (1 Cor. 1, 2; 2 Cor. 1, 1), even the small Christian community or neighborhood circle which was accustomed to come together in the house of an individual (Rom. 16, 5; 1 Cor. 16, 19; Col. 4, 15; Phil. 2), received the title "ἐκκλησία": the community assembled by the loving call of God. The universal Church is in no small measure a perceptible and visible brotherhood in these living cells.

The desire for unity and brotherhood has been placed in the hearts of men by the common Creator and Father; brotherhood was brought into the world by Christ in a new manner of reality surpassing all human concepts and offered to us as a genuine possibility. This knowledge of a final and profound solidarity and unity has formed the soul of Western man through a thousand years. But when piety began to be merely more or less a concern of the isolated individual, and when the clergy, as a socially entrenched class, defended its privileges along with other monopolistic groups, when men in the Church separated themselves into groups with a frighteningly good conscience and thought only of themselves and their groups, the French Revolution for the first time gave the word "brotherhood" (fraternité) a purely secular meaning. And finally, the most powerful prophet of this world, Karl Marx, understood how to address this hidden longing of men created for unity in Christ, this most profound spiritual yearning of the suppressed working class. Because Christian brotherhood seemed to be forgotten, a Satanic image could erect itself in the collective of Communism. There is no other way to liberate humanity from the slavery of the collective and from mass culture than the rediscovered Christian brotherhood, the φιλ-αδελφία, which Jesus brought to us; and in order to accomplish this Jesus continues to live in his Church.

The Newness of the Moral Life

All slogans are probably one-sided and inexact. Precision is generally sacrificed for a striking effect. This is also true of the formula current today—"Christianity as an experience of new life." For this reason we will show here that a moral life emanating from the strength of Christian faith and rebirth is indeed something essentially new; and how, on the other hand, this newness can be made known effectively and circumspectly to the new Christians in the mission lands and likewise to new converts in our traditionally Christian lands.

Let us first of all ask Christ himself and the apostle to the gentiles, Paul, how they proclaimed the good news of the new life. From this we will learn how we can escape the danger of falsifying or disguising the new experience. For it is from this correct contact with the ethos of the contemporary spiritual milieu, to which the proclamation of the Church must appeal concretely, that new vital forms of Christian morality can and will result.

THE NEWNESS OF THE MORAL LIFE IN THE MORAL PREACHING OF CHRIST AND ST. PAUL

Christ, speaking as "One who has power," stressed with great clarity the newness of his good tidings and, closely interwoven with it, the newness of his moral challenge. But the new message that he proclaims does not mean a breach with that which God made known to the chosen people in the Old Covenant. The new rather joins on to the old everywhere. "Think not that I have come to abolish the law and the prophets; I have come not to abolish them but to fulfill them" (Mt. 5, 17).

What is new is not the commandment of love; even in the Old Covenant that was already the synopsis of the Law. But the revelation of that which the love of God gives us in this time of saving fullness is new: "For God so loved the world that he gave his only Son" (Jn. 3, 16). What is new is therefore the basis and the measure of love: "A new commandment I give to you, that you love one another; even as I have loved you, that you also love one another" (Jn. 13, 34; 15, 12ff.).

Although Christ does connect his message to the Old Testament revelation, he emphasizes sharply the newness of his message of the true conversion of heart, of the full divine dominion over the hearts of men and over all provinces of life *in contrast* to the Pharisaical law which cramps and alienates through an exaggerated legalistic morality of don'ts. Here he repeats time after time: "You have heard . . . , but I say to you" (Mt. 5, 21 to 6, 16).

Thus the divine Master leads the circle of disciples to experience the newness of the moral life through the intimate connection of his moral message with what had already been revealed to them earlier by the gracious will of God, and through the sharp confrontation with the symptoms of degeneration against which the good in man has always to some degree struggled.

Because Christ himself preached essentially only to the lost lamb of Israel, we must also ask Paul, the great apostle to the gentiles, how he handed on to the gentiles the new things which Christ had announced to the sons of the chosen people. The apostle to the gentiles is passionately concerned not to allow the newness of the good news and particularly of the moral message

30

to be concealed. With an unequaled ardor he battles every attempt of the Judaizers to obscure the good news of salvation and of life in Christ by their intolerant dissemination of Jewish customs and Old Testament statutes.

Paul recognizes the natural good in the gentile world (see Rom. 2, 14f.; 1, 32). He praises the great piety of the Athenians who erected an altar to the unknown god (Acts 17, 22f.). He alludes especially to their never-fading longing for deliverance. But at the same time he sharply contrasts the demands of the new life of those delivered through Christ and reborn in Christ to the depravity of the heathen milieu. Thus Paul believes the experience of newness in the Christian faith and the Christian moral teaching is not compromised by being joined with the good that lives in the gentile peoples. But he does see the newness of this life greatly endangered by the overemphasis on the statutory (the external legality) and by the introduction of Jewish details into gentile communities.

To him, what is new is the divine dominion breaking through in Christ, in the love which God has given men in Christ. The moral life is to him, as it is in the entire New Testament, a part of the good news. The new does not consist of some kind of performance of what is demanded by law; it is nothing other than "the law of the Spirit of life in Christ Jesus" (Rom. 8, 2). The Christian as a new creature is neither anarchist nor subject of a law coming to him purely from without; he bears the law within himself through the very life given him by the Holy Spirit in Christ Jesus (1 Cor. 1, 29). But for this reason the Christian must also lead a new life in all things and purge the old leaven of sin. The new life, which Paul preaches constantly and urgently to the self-righteous Pharisees and Judaizers as well as to the anthropocentric Greeks and Romans, sees the moral life within the perspective of the gracious loving will of God. The Jew caught in the briers of legalistic casuistry discovers something completely new in Paul, just as the gentile oriented to external formalities and to mere human wisdom discovers the wonderful unity of faith and moral life, of the saving mystery (*mysterium*) and the formation of life: between the working of God's grace and the love fulfilling and reaching out towards men from God.

It is the shockingly new within the love of God which reveals itself in the death on the cross of the only-begotten Son of God, the incomprehensibly new of the humility of the condescending God, which Paul consciously and constantly attempts to place in the center of his apostolic preaching (see 1 Cor. 1, 17; 2, 2f.). From this very concept he derives the law and the motivation of the new life: "It is no longer I who live, but Christ who lives in me; and the life I now live in the flesh I live by faith in the Son of God, who loved me and gave himself for me" (Gal. 2, 20). "And walk in love, as Christ loved us" (Eph. 5, 2). "In all these things we are more than conquerors through him who loved us" (Rom. 8, 37; see 1 Jn. 4, 19). "We love, because he first loved us."[1]

The preaching of the cross forms a whole with the Easter message of the resurrection. From this preaching of the cross, so scandal-provoking to the Greeks, and from the resurrection of the human body, Paul derives the new ethos in reference to the body: ". . . always carrying in the body the death of Jesus, so that the life of Jesus may also be manifested in our bodies" (2 Cor. 4, 10). "So glorify God in your body" (1 Cor. 6, 20).

THE DANGER OF ADULTERATING AND OBSCURING THE NEW

Paul did not wish to bring Jewish forms of life to the gentiles, nor did he demand a universal abrupt breaking off of their traditional way of life. He himself wished in his exterior form

[1] See B. Häring, *The Law of Christ*, volume II, Westminster, 1964, pp. 351ff.

of life to be all things to all men, a Jew to the Jews, to the gentiles as one from their midst (1 Cor. 9, 20ff.). The reason was not only that the foreign form of life would be for many an obstacle to conversion—though Paul did take that into consideration, too, and for that reason, for example, he allowed Timothy to be circumcised out of concern for the mission to the Jews—but another chief reason was his knowledge that man is easily fascinated by externals and could mistake the unfamiliar new forms of life for the essentials of the new doctrine and the new life. The defenders of Jewish legalism were indeed ordinarily men who, because of the externals of the old Law, were unable to put the comforting new things of the redemption by Christ and the new life of the reborn into focus. The apostle to the gentiles, who in self-forgetfulness and self-renunciation became everything to everyone, did at one point refuse to accommodate himself: he wished to preach to the Greeks, so proud of their wisdom, "not with eloquent wisdom, lest the cross of Christ be emptied of its power" (1 Cor. 1, 17). He accommodated himself to the simple little people. Of course, that does not mean that he did not discuss the Greek philosophy or the ethics of the Stoa. He certainly did, extensively. And the early Christian Fathers discussed it with all imaginable thoroughness. Our Western predecessors received along with the Christian good news a rich load of Greek and Roman culture of which we need not be ashamed today. But missionizing has a duty not to Greek philosophy and not to Roman jurisprudence, but rather first to the divine grace of a genuine adaptation to the individuality of the mission lands. When the young peoples of the European continent, like the tribally related Anglo-Saxons, were so quickly and thoroughly won to Christianity, it was due in no small part to a genial missionary accommodation on the part of the great heralds of faith.

It is a real danger for the Christian teaching on the moral life when we proclaim it to cultures of completely different background in the categories of Aristotle, of the Stoa, of one of the two scholastics of the same stamp, or even in the garments of the old Roman or typical modern and Western jurisprudence. A very intelligent and sincere Vietnamese priest once told us that to him the teaching of Confucius still seemed more stirring and preferable to a *manuale theologiae moralis* of which three-fourths is legal casuistry while the rest is presented in more or less juristic form. When we became somewhat skeptical of this criticism of the Latin textbooks on moral theology which had been introduced into East Asia, the young Vietnamese would not rest until we had read the four holy books of Confucianism[2] thoroughly and had declared to him that moral theology can indeed build upon them more easily than on Stoic ethics or Western legal thought. When in the thought of Confucius, for example, we find at the summit of the "basic virtues given to us by heaven" goodness, or benevolence, it is really incomprehensible why we, particularly in Asia, should rest with the Greek schema after we have once been made aware that the Greeks did not have as high an interpretation of love. Whereas in the thought of Confucius love is the highest gift of heaven, and it alone is able to establish a correct order within the heart, to the Greeks it was only a passion or an effort towards one's own fulfillment.

It is clear that we must also ponder Christian moral teaching in the scholarly categories of Western ethics and draw it into a systematic presentation. But even in the proclamation in our own cultural circle we somehow run the risk of obscuring what is intrinsic to the Christian life, the Good News of the gracious dominion of God, by our "eloquent wisdom." The danger is so much the greater when we bring a part of the Stoa, Aristotle, or Gratian to the Indians, Chinese, Japanese, or Africans and do

[2] The four holy books can be found in French and Latin translation by S. Couveur, S.J., in *Les quatre livres*, H. Kiou Fou, 1895.

34

not clearly distinguish what is the essential Christian message and what the Western addition or form.

A further danger in the proclamation of the Christian message to the gentiles, one to which the holy apostle Paul also makes us attentive, is the mixing of our own historically qualified ethos with the enduring and essential demands of the Christian religion. Even a comparison of the scholarly works of moral theology from various centuries can give us an idea of how greatly the mores conditioned by the milieu, the merely customary usage, can change, and how these customs are sometimes enjoined even by recognized scholars in the same tone as the enduring demands following from the nature of man or the Christian faith. Only a basic thinking through of our moral teaching and a fundamental study of the sources, of the holy Scriptures and the Church Fathers, can protect us from demanding as an enduring requirement of the moral life from the newly converted what in reality is only a time-conditioned precept or a more or less variable manifestation of an essential Christian demand.

THE NEWNESS OF MORALITY AND THE NEWNESS OF CUSTOMS

Customs and usages form in certain respects an over-all expression of the religious, moral, and cultural levels of a community.[3] Only the man who has a sympathetic understanding of the whole can correctly judge the totality of customs and usages as well as individual manifestations. It would be dangerous for young Christian communities in mission lands, and especially dangerous for isolated Christians who have not yet been able to experience the good fortune of a supporting and sustaining Christian com-

[3] This must not in any way be understood to mean that customs and usages can be compared only slightly with morality or even with religion. We are concerned here only with a causality of expression.

munity, if the Christian life demanded a sudden and radical break with the customs of the milieu. Once again we can learn from the apostle to the gentiles. In the Letter to the Romans he admonishes "the strong" who, from the absolutely correct insight that the old Jewish food restrictions no longer had validity, drew without further deliberation the obvious inference of nonobservance; through this they gave scandal which endangered the salvation of the Jewish Christians still weak in the faith (Rom. 14-15). Paul counts himself among the strong who think no food is impure (Rom. 14, 14). But the deciding factor must be not this knowledge, but the loving concern for the salvation of the weak and for the spreading of the gospel. So the new freedom must sometimes be foregone for a time. Would it not be a good thing to show the new Christians in mission lands that, out of loving concern for the propagating of the faith but also out of love of what is their own, they should hold to many old customs, although they must at the same time be completely aware that these customs in themselves present no enduring law of morality—provided, of course, that the custom represented as binding until this time does not present something in itself evil?

The "incident of Antioch" (the argument of Paul with Peter in Gal. 2, 11ff.) shows on the other hand a situation in which the excessive concern of Peter for the sensitivity of Jewish Christians threatened to endanger the mission to the gentiles. That Peter himself did not evaluate the situation correctly and had to let himself be instructed by Paul is, moreover, an example of how difficult it is to judge correctly whether certain customs and mores should or should not be left behind. The *strong* Christians in Corinth had carried the adaptation too far when, following their own insight into the nullity, the nonexistence, of the heathen gods, they calmly went to the market and bought meat sacrificed to them. The time when such a procedure could be an effective and open witness against the null gods had not yet come. Instead, this way of acting gave occasion to those still wavering in the faith to insure themselves with the old gods, too.

In all these questions and cases of adaptation the holy apostle Paul emphatically states the decisive and new element in the moral message of Christianity: "Decide never to put a stumbling block or hindrance in the way of a brother!" (Rom. 14, 13). "Let no one seek his own good, but the good of his neighbor" (1 Cor. 10, 24).

The question whether adhering to certain traditional customs is compatible with the new Christian life, whether or not it facilitates the effective proclamation of the Christian teaching and of the Christian life, will always have to be judged anew for every place and for every time. What is important is that the valid standard which Paul exhibits so effectively never be forgotten. It is in this time-conditioned and often burning question that the Christian should recognize the new truth—in the fact that it is not concerned with usage, especially not the suppression of one's own inherited form of life or even the introduction of a custom foreign to the people, that neither the inherited nor the strange nor even the statutory has meaning of itself, but rather that love alone and its expression suitable to the matter and the time is decisive.

Paul instructs the Christians in a still heathen milieu: "Conduct yourselves wisely" (Col. 4, 5), become a part of the milieu wisely and shrewdly, as far as that is possible without betrayal of the truth. Good sense as well as love demands this. Everything appropriate and virtuous should be retained by Christians (Phil. 4, 8). The missionary fitting-in with the customs conditioned by the milieu and order of society conforms also to the warning of Paul to all members of the Christian community to persevere in the exterior form of life in which the gospel reached them. What is more, he applies this to the slaves. "So, brethren, in whatever state each was called, there let him remain with God" (1 Cor. 7, 24). Nevertheless, where "wise conduct" vis-à-vis the world permits it, the slave should not reject the possibility of emancipation (1 Cor. 7, 21).

The newness of Christian morality must from the very beginning come to new Christians with all possible strength and be brought to the consciousness of the new Christians as a life lived out of the grace given them. But for that reason the new must not be concealed by foreign schemas, philosophical categories, or time-conditioned statutes which likewise can seem novel. Above all, the new life must not be buried under a mass of old or new positive precepts.

All attempts at forming a Christian life will in the long run be hopeless if they proceed essentially from the exterior and external. The first thing is to proclaim the good news, to awaken joy, to deepen faith, to initiate and vivify the community of faith and cult. From this follow with intrinsic necessity the great and strong impulses of a new form of life and a gradual penetration of the community with the spirit of Christianity. This is not only confirmed by the nature of Christian religion and every truly religious morality, but it is also widely supported empirically.[4] Everything which seems at any given time to be necessary in its external protective and legal form must be based on ultimate principles, but certainly not in such a way that the danger of an absolutizing of transitory and cultural forms could be charged to it.

If obsolete or foreign social mores are held onto or introduced, or if the earlier time-conditioned forms of customs and usages cannot be animated by love, examined and relegated to their rightful place, then the Church of a particular place will lose its ability to mold and remold genuine cultural forms of customs and usages. It is part of the newness of the Christian life in the Church that it presents itself in ever new rich forms of customs, usages, and culture. The Christian religion is so fertile and

[4] See B. Häring, *Macht und Ohnmacht der Religion. Religionssoziologie als Anruf*, Salzburg, 1956, pp. 38–43; 92ff.; 284ff.

creative that her treasures can be found only in variety, and only in variety are all her creative possibilities fulfilled. As the splendor of the Christian life is seen in the varied lives of the saints, so too it must come to light ever anew in varied cultures and in new stylistic forms.

The Upheaval in Moral Theology

EVER since moral theology began to constitute a proper theological discipline there has been continual vigorous discussion and open self-criticism within the field. But its self-analysis has perhaps never before extended to essence, sources, methods, and goal as much as it does today. The casuistic-canonical type of *institutiones theologiae moralis* (moral textbooks) which were oriented towards the "court of penance," and which on the whole were uncontested for three centuries, has begun to waver for the first time, and seriously. Today a series of compelling factors has brought the apparently benumbed forms of moral theology to the thawing point in almost all countries. Probably most important among these factors are the present-day Bible movement, the newly deepened relation to the liturgical-sacramental life, and the dynamic character of modern society. The *entire* meaning of the diverse and yet converging efforts towards the renewal of the Catholic presentation of the Christian life can be indicated here only in the most essential outlines.

MORAL THEOLOGY IN THE UPHEAVAL OF THE TIMES

The progress of technology and the natural sciences, especially modern medicine, psychotherapy, the changes of economic structures, new forms of private and communal property, the modern means of propagating opinion and forming collective goals—all these present moral theology with so many different problems of a new and difficult sort that it can no longer afford to squander time and strength on sterile "exercise cases." But much more than new individual problems is involved; the question is being raised whether we can be just to these new problems with the tools of the post-Tridentine morality of the confessional, or whether the very abundance of the new questions does not demand a new synthesis, a new over-all view. Added to this is perhaps the most decisive factor—that the majority of the faithful today live in what is in every respect a pluralistic society. Catholics, at least those who follow the Catholic system of values, almost everywhere form a minority. The situation in Rome, San Francisco, Paris, or Munich is not much different from that in New York, London, Berlin, or Tokyo. The modern Catholic no longer lives in a secluded Catholic area. Even if there is still here and there a Catholic village or a Catholic town with an outwardly genuine traditional Christianity to which everyone more or less conforms, the secular world of a much different nature sends its spirit there in a thousand impulses; and the antennae for the reception of this other message are not lacking. Added to this, the enormous mobility of modern society throws people from the most remote village on the shore of another world. Here the task of today's pastoral sociology begins. It shows how shockingly ineffectual mere moral imperatives are, for the morally immature man, no longer carried along by a Christian society, is thrown into confusion before the vital strength of a non-Christian system of values. John L. Thomas, S.J.,[1] draws from the great amount of sociological research on the situation of the Catholic family in the United States one main conclusion: the times demand a complete rethinking of Catholic marriage and family morality; the Catholic position

[1] *The American Catholic Family,* Englewood Cliffs, 1956.

must be presented constructively and contrasted to the ideals predominating today; it must show itself capable of realizing its own ideals in the midst of the essentially different social conditions of today. In closed Catholic societies—and these are what the "classical moral textbooks" had in mind—it was sufficient to enumerate in some way individual norms and individual duties. The changing situation of today demands above all else a deep foundation and comprehensive presentation of that which is Christian. *The experience of the new life* which the old Christian moral proclamation emphasized is no less important today.

MORAL THEOLOGY AND LAW

One of the chief accusations against moral theology of the past three centuries (particularly that of the French writers), is the partial "legalization" of morals. Up to this very day many works bear the proud title *Moral Theology* with the addition "according to the norms of canon law" or "with special consideration of canon and civil law." Legal casuistry not seldom makes up to nine-tenths of all the material, and what is even more serious— purely moral-theological questions are treated primarily according to the method of legal science, whose chief attention is centered on pushing the limits of general duties down towards the legal minimum.

A few things might be said in defense of our forefathers: They had to perforce occupy themselves more with canon law, for there was no comprehensive *Codex Juris Canonici* (the ecclesiastical law book since 1918), and well-formed professors of Church law were everywhere wanting.

Law, even Church law, has first of all a function to conserve, to fence in the rules solidified through history. It is a social power of regulation which must prevent the disintegration of the community. It can, however, also become a danger if it is oriented towards *yesterday* instead of *today*. For as we live through this

43

era, one of the most vital in the world's history, moral theology must work out the positive contribution of law to morals and morality. Even law itself would lose the flexibility necessary for genuine adaptation to completely new circumstances, and—what is even more important—moral teaching would seem unbelievable to modern man if moral theology tried to appear today in the form of a code of law formulated once for all. This is so much the more obvious at the present moment as the Church herself prepares to undertake a basic revision of her legislation.

This is not a question of mere utility. There are deeper reasons forbidding Catholic moral theology to present itself so to speak as a mere catalogue of commandments and restrictions; but the uniquely dynamic society of our time is with reason in favor of an examination of conscience by today's moral theology; it recognizes more and more that an excess of canon law material or the imitation of legal science in its methods will necessarily veil its uniqueness and destroy the experience of newness which surpasses that of every other system.

THE LAW OF GRACE

The basic demand of Christian morality says: *Live from the grace you have received.* But grace is a stimulus to constant growth. The gracious call of Christ to follow him, the beatitudes, the chief commandment of love, the sacramental assimilation to Christ, the eschatological hope—in short, everything that is an unmistakable mark of New Testament morality—demands an incessant struggle for the heights, a constant deepening of conversion, a more and more intimate turning towards Christ and the concerns of his kingdom. The Christian life, then, is of incomparably greater movement and vitality than our society of today. This being called by grace and this being drawn towards the goal are simply not expressible in the language of law, not even of church law. The same dynamic of grace which urges individual Christians towards growth in love is also a law of the Christian community. The kingdom of heaven in this time of pilgrimage is "like a little mustard seed" which must grow. The community of Christ may never show herself satisfied with her interior life or her success in Christianizing society. The violent upheaval of the time makes it easy for us to overlook the fact that even in the past we have never had an absolutely Christian society. It was never more than a prospect, a remote approach.

Legal thinking is content to preserve a minimum, to entrench what is already attained. In times of stability, genuine Christian *élan* attempts a continual deepening and intensification; but in times of upheaval it ventures a new scheme and attempts to inform anew whatever is Christian in the changing world, knowing that this is possible only if the source is pure and strong.

The regaining of positive commandments, in contrast to the casuistry which defines moral boundaries, as a center of gravity stands out clearly in today's moral theology. Casuistry itself acquires a new form in an application directed towards growth, towards a constructive over-all plan instead of towards merely defensive attitudes. Many tendencies in today's moral theology give us hope that the principally corrective morality of minimums will finally take place for a more courageous beginning, a forward direction, a life form never content with itself. The new emphasis on the law of grace as a law of growth, and the interest in social problems which can recognize the "*kairós*" (the granted right moment) fosters this hope. The all too bourgeois attitudes must yield to the eschatological virtues of vigilance, hope, daring.

With few restrictions one can indeed say: Moral theology the world over is setting about loosening its excessively close relationship with law. The Pauline understanding of the "law of

45

grace," the taking up once again of the teaching of perfection, which for a long time had been handed down apart from morality, especially in ascetics and mysticism, a stronger and closer alliance to dogma and liturgy, and an articulate social-welfare-thinking help moral theology to the *distinguishing of that which is Christian* so necessary today. From this then a deeper consciousness of the moral-theological basis of law and a fruitful meeting with the world of today are also possible.

The Doctrine of the Kingdom of God

The classic treatise on the "proximate occasion of sin," which in the *institutiones theologiae moralis* not seldom carried with it a certain odor of salvation individualism, is, of course, not attacked by today's moral theology. Nevertheless, it does broaden itself out to a more positive view of activity in the world. The same is true of the treatise on "material cooperation." The vast revolution of the lay apostolate has led to a theology of the lay state and worldly realities. The tormented individualistic question "How do I assure myself of a gracious God?", or "How do I save my soul?", has again given way to the broad biblical view: "The kingdom of God has come."

In moral theology, especially in view of the milieu in which the laity must work, the fundamental question and the ultimate motive becomes the grateful consciousness of being seized by the kingdom of God and being permitted and charged to act for the kingdom of God. Just as a more and more constructive *care of souls living in the world* prevails in pastoral theology,[2] so too moral theology is turning to all the related questions with a more positive attitude. It is not only social ethics which receives more and more treatment and weight, but also the basic questions of general moral theology: moral perception, freedom, conscience, sin, conversion and growth in virtue are receiving

[2] See V. Schurr, *Konstruktive Seelsorge*, Freiburg, 1963.

in increasing measure a strong social salvation accent. The strivings and struggles of the Christian again stand more clearly in the perspective of the salvation history of the people of God. The doctrine of the last things is no longer put forward only as a motive for concern for one's own soul. The battle at the end of time between the forces of the kingdom of God and the forces of perdition, the crucifixion, the resurrection, the ascension, and second coming of Christ again become forceful motives for a *communal* Christian hope, a communal concern for salvation, a common labor to Christianize the world. The connection between the freedom of the children of God and the groaning of creation for the manifestation of this freedom is again seen clearly. Systematic moral theology is at least seriously striving to build this view of the Christian life.

THE CHRISTOCENTRIC PERSPECTIVE

The kingdom of God is in our midst through Christ. Through his incarnation, his death, and his resurrection, Christ has brought us the delivering royal dominion of his Father. He has ascended the throne of glory at the right hand of the Father that from there he might send us the Holy Spirit to make his Church, his disciples into living personal tools of his saving dominion. Through his church, in the strength of his Holy Spirit, Christ himself is "the way, the truth, and the life" (Jn. 14, 6). He is himself the law of Christians through his Spirit which gives us his life, which intensifies in us his word and his example and teaches us to understand and obey the doctrines and wisdom of the church in unity with the law of grace written in the heart.

The passionate concern of the apostle of the gentiles is that the Christian life should not stand first of all under an external law. "The law of Christ" (Gal. 6, 2) is the love of God which has come to us in a completely personal way in Christ, which

47

urges us from within to love our neighbor with Christ and in Christ. "The law of grace," "the law of faith," "the primacy of love"—all these central truths are thought through again today in the spirit of St. Paul and often with a passion reminiscent of him, with an invocation of the great fathers of the church, especially Augustine and Thomas Aquinas, and of the One in their midst, of Christ.

An accentuated christocentric presentation of all theology, but especially of moral theology, will perhaps be one of the happiest results of the Second Vatican Council. This view was stressed by Paul VI in continuing the line of his predecessor in the address at the beginning of the second session: "Christ! Christ our starting point. Christ our way and leader. Christ our hope and goal. May the council give full attention to this complex yet simple, stable and at the same time dynamic, mysterious and crystal clear, forceful and felicitous relationship between us and Jesus, the most blessed, between this holy and living Church, which we are, and Christ, from whom we come, for whom we live and to whom we go. No light should shine on this assembly that is not Christ the light of the world; no truth other than the words of the Lord our only Master should interest us; no other goal should urge us on than the desire to be unconditionally loyal to him. . . . In the language of the liturgy we wish to say: 'We know you Christ, you alone; we seek you with a pure and simple heart.' "

Christocentric moral theology of today joins the *personal* characteristics with the *mystic-sacramental* and the *social salvation-ecclesiological*. Christian personalism in the moral theology of today is not to be understood as self-sufficient or self-seeking efforts towards its own perfection. On the other hand, it also does not make the person subject to a dead literal law. Christ himself in his person makes known the will of his Father; he calls each man by name and invites him to follow him. But the personal relation to Christ may not in any way be looked upon

48

as a merely external confrontation, as an answer to an exterior call. The decisive factor is the sacramental-mystical basis: Christ lives *in us*. Of course, Fritz Tillmann's basic idea, "the following of Christ,"[3] experienced some criticism and rebuttal in the beginning from numerous theologians, especially those writing in the Romance languages, who equated following with exterior imitation. But these very controversies—not least under the influence of the liturgical-sacramental movement—led to a deeper understanding of the basic concepts of following, especially of "being-in-Christ." *Being-in-Christ* means at the same time the most complete relationship of the entire person to Christ and membership in his mystical body, the Church, and in conformity with this a personal relation of love and solidarity with each member of the body of Christ.

SACRAMENTAL MORAL THEOLOGY

Under the influence of the liturgical renewal moral theology of today has again become conscious that the Church Fathers almost always presented Christian ethics in conjunction with sacramental instruction. A classical example is the mystagogical catechesis of St. Cyril (or, as was earlier supposed, John) of Jerusalem. In scholasticism, too, up until Bonaventure, the moral theological treatises follow after the salvation history truths of creation, incarnation, or, most often, the teaching on the sacraments. In the moral textbooks of the past three hundred years, the sacraments were for the first time treated apart as their own sphere of duty, and in fact usually after the commandments. Here Church law stipulations respecting the reception and administration of the sacraments received the greatest treatment. Scarcely one of these books mentions that the sacraments confer

[3] Fritz Tillmann (editor), *Handbuch der katholischen Sittenlehre*, volume III: Tillmann, *Die Idee der Nachfolge Christi*, Düsseldorf, 1953; volume IV: Tillmann, *Die Verwirklichung der Nachforlge Christi*, Düsseldorf, 1950.

along with new life the divine commission for a life to be lived in the spirit of Christ and in the community of redemption. The doctrine on the sacraments was presented in a legalistic-positivistic way, while the presentation of the moral life seemed to use only the categories of external duty or the commandment of natural law. The characteristic feature of New Testament law as a law of grace, as the "spiritual law of the life in Christ Jesus," was slighted proportionately as the sacraments represented only an additional sphere of duty.

The *liturgical movement* has pushed the sacred mysteries back into the center of the Christian form of existence. The liturgical renewal which began so vigorously in the time of St. Pius X has not, as some moralistic critics predicted, degenerated to an esthetic or formalistic affair. It has in no way weakened moral activity and the effective apostolate, but rather has proved itself more and more a means and source of strength for a truly supernatural life and a communal apostolate of the faithful emanating from the altar. Perhaps this will prove the death-blow to the *moralism* resulting from humanism and the Enlightenment.

Because the generation of moral theologians rising today has been formed from youth on by the liturgical movement, scientific moral theology is also gaining a new over-all perspective. Although so deserving a scholar of the moral theological renewal as Fritz Tillmann could still cram teaching on the sacraments under the heading "Die Pflichten gegen sich selbst im Bereich des Religiösen"[4] ("Duties towards Oneself in Religious Matters"), energetic attempts to present the sacramental life as the source and norm of the total moral formation are finding today almost common approbation. That is, however, possible only because the sacraments are again understood more consciously as a personal claim on grace, as a common saving gift of grace and a

[4] Fritz Tillmann, "Die Pflichten gegen sich selbst im Bereich des Religiösen," in *Die Verwirklichung der Nachfolge Christi.*

common saving summons. The view, prevailing frequently in the past centuries, of the sacraments as "means of grace for the fulfillment of the moral law," reorders itself to the christocentric, theocentric perspective. The sacred mysteries hallow our life, place it in the radiance of the holiness of God. Thus the virtue of divine worship, together with the supernatural virtues, which are also presented in a more personal-dialogical way, becomes a comprehensive formal principle of moral theology.

The meaning of the liturgy for the Christian formation of life is expressly emphasized by the splendid constitution of the Second Vatican Council from the first word on. The Introduction begins: "This sacred Council has several aims in view: it desires to impart an ever increasing vigor to the Christian life of the faithful; . . . For the liturgy, 'through which the work of our redemption is accomplished,' most of all in the divine sacrifice of the eucharist, is the outstanding means whereby the faithful may express in their lives, and manifest to others, the mystery of Christ and the real nature of the true Church." With the unanimous acceptance and proclamation of this constitution, the sacramental and at the same time christocentric orientation of moral theology has experienced a magnificent confirmation.

The conciliar *Constitution on the Sacred Liturgy* succeeded in assuring the Easter mystery, with its wonderful unity of death and resurrection, ascension and Parousia of the Lord, an absolutely central place not only in the understanding of the liturgy itself, but also, emanating from it, in the over-all understanding of the Christian life. Worship is seen as Pentecostal by the anointing by the Spirit of Christ. Thus the permanent introduction into the "law of the Spirit" is also assured by the liturgical disposition.

The *Dogmatic Constitution on the Church* builds further in the same direction. The Church understands itself as *mysterium*, as the proto-sacrament of the encounter with Christ. The entire people of God experiences a deeper conviction of faith from the wider operation of the priestly office of Christ. The clearer emergence of collegiality in the understanding of the primacy and the episcopal office opens a more vital approach from the priesthood into the primacy of love. With the best of reasons one may allow himself to hope that the *spirit of worship* will animate and invigorate everything in the Church anew.

Moral theology is on the move. Unless everything deceives us, the result may be a greater fidelity to the total Catholic tradition. Fidelity to tradition demands more than a mere handing on of formulas. A deeper digging for the sources, a more immediate contact with the saving mystery, a more passionate encounter with the eternal truth in the stress of the times will also create the suppositions for a more just and loving judgment on earlier theologians, who will now no longer be judged by their formulas but by their *salvific service to their time.*[5]

[5] See F. Böckle, "Bestrebungen in der Moraltheologie," in *Fragen der Theologie heute,* volume II, Einsiedeln, 1957, pp. 425–446; A. Auer, "Anliegen heutiger Moraltheologie, in *Theol. Quartalschr.,* 138, 1958, pp. 275–305; G. Ermecke, "Die katholische Moraltheologie heute," in *Theologie und Glaube,* 1951, pp. 127–142; S. Pinckaers, "Le renouveau de la théologie morale," in *La Vie Intellectuelle,* 27, October, 1956, pp. 1–21; P. Delhaye, "Die gegenwärtigen Bestrebungen der Moraltheologie in Frankreich," in *Moralprobleme im Umbruch der Zeit,* edited by V. Redlich, Munich, 1957, pp. 13–39; E. Meersch, "La morale et le Christ total," in *Nouv. Rev. Théol.,* 68, 1946, pp. 633–647; J. Fuchs, "Die Liebe als Aufbauprinzip der Moraltheologie," in *Scholastik,* 29, 1954, pp. 79–87; T. Steinbüchel, *Religion und Moral im Lichte christlicher Existenz,* Frankfurt, 1961; J. Leclercq, *Christliche Moral in der Krise der Zeit,* Einsiedeln, 1954; F.–M. Braun and C. Spicq, *Morale chrétienne et requêtes contemporaines,* Tournai, 1954; B. Häring, *Das Heilige und das Gute. Religion und Sittlichkeit in ihrem gegenseitigen Bezug,* Freiburg, Wewel, 1950, and *The Law of Christ,* volumes I and II.

Is the Moral Theology of St. Alphonsus Relevant?

BY an apostolic brief of April 26, 1950, Pius XII declared St. Alphonsus of Liguori[1] "the heavenly patron of all priests who exercise the exceedingly important and salutary office of confessor, and of all those who serve by word and pen the communication of moral theology."[2]

Even this solemn manifestation—to say nothing of the many other utterances of the apostolic see in this regard—makes clear that the Church is convinced of the relevance and value as a model of the moral theology of St. Alphonsus. In what does this relevance lie, and what does it mean for us in so different a time?

In order to attain a fundamental view of the relevance of earlier theologians and the doctors of the Church, we will call to mind first of all the relevance of the word of God so that by analogy to it we may grasp more concretely the relevance of St. Alphonsus for his time and for our time.

1. The Relevance of the Word of God

The word of God, written down in the holy Scriptures, meant first of all and immediately a completely concrete, unsurpassably

[1] This essay was given in a somewhat shorter form at a public lecture at the beginning of the academic year 1960–1961 on the occasion of the insertion of the Academia Alfonsiana into the theological faculty of the Lateran University.

[2] *AAS*, 42, 1950, p. 595.

relevant call for the people to whom it was immediately addressed. It had its direct and first relevance *"in illo tempore"* (ἐν ἐκείνῳ τῷ χαιρῷ), in that particular hour of salvation. The commission given along with the Good News lives in the eternally valid truth, but it is concretized for these men in this precise surrounding and in these very special gifts of grace.

When the Church proclaims the Gospel to us today with the stereotyped introduction *"in illo tempore,"* does this mean that the word of God is not also proclaimed to this our present hour? Yes, it is, but not simply, not without a detour through the simple men listening to the salvific events "at that time." The word of God is relevant to every time. In the most immediate fashion it is relevant here and now (ἐν τούτῳ τῷ χαιρῷ) through the eternal validity of the truth which it proclaims and by its value as a model for the particular hour of salvation.

The Church as the Channel of the Relevance of the Word of God

The community of salvation to which the word of God is entrusted and which is to proclaim it for that time always remains the same: the one, holy, apostolic, and catholic Church. But the Church is not monotonous and uniform; in her very abundance she is rich and beautiful—and relevant. She is the One Thing in the development of salvation history which is constantly involved in a new becoming-flesh (incarnation) in various cultures and times.

The Adventists and all sectarian biblical students do not take the pains to explore patiently the precise original meaning of holy Scripture by studying the biblical environment and language. They take the word of God only as a word to one individual here and now. From this follow their superficial attempts to construct an unbridgeable opposition between holy Scripture and the Church of today. It is not only that they wish to undevelop the tree which has grown up out of the "little mustard seed" in two thousand years and return it to the form of a one-year-old seedling. They fail to see the problem of salvation history as one of the dominion and word of God being present for every time in constantly new relevance.

The exact sociological and psychological situation into which the biblical passage was spoken and in which it was written down is investigated by Catholic exegesis with the utmost conscientiousness with the aid of a great number of tools. That is not all: It never forgets at the same time that it is the living Church of today which vitally transmits the word of God, proclaims it anew to every time, and preserves the unfalsified relevance of the word of God in the very fact that she proclaims it to every time in its own language and for its own needs.

Certainly, the original concreteness of the word of God corresponding to the various literary forms of the individual books and parts of holy Scripture has various degrees of concretization and relevance for the very special conditions "at that time." But it is always true that anyone who wishes to recognize the eternal, unalterable truth that is contained in holy Scripture and in the witness of the early Church without acknowledging the relevance of the word of God for his own particular hour of salvation, does not even understand correctly that which is eternal in the truth, because he does not make the effort to distinguish between the eternally valid declaration of truth and the concrete style of the declaration. In addition, he blunts the relevance of the word of God for our time. For only when we see how immediately men of that time were affected by the word of God do we let ourselves be just as relevantly affected in our own situation, often so completely different.

In the face of an existentialism bogged down in the unstructured, we hold that the great ideas of the philosophers thousands of years away are intelligible and comprehensible; but at the same time, we do not forget that a correct understanding of earlier thinkers, even of the most abstract of all thinkers, presupposes great efforts of philosophico-historical research. Even the philosopher constantly in some way thought and spoke in dialogue with his time.

It is not true that the word of God, because it infinitely surpasses the thought of all philosophers in eternally valid truth, therefore bears less the character of historical relevance. The more it surpasses human wisdom in eternal validity, the greater is its relevance in the concreteness of salvation history. That means, of course, a deep condescension on the part of the God speaking to us, a sharing in the *exinanitio* (renunciation) of the Word of God in Person in the incarnation.

Scripture and Tradition

Theology, which is an ecclesiastical service to the proclamation of the word of God, partakes of the relevance of the word of God in its own way. Theology is no mere handing on of the words of holy Scripture; it is living tradition (*traditio viva*), a most relevant saving service, for it is the science of salvation. Theology is never established once for all in systems of words and concepts which could be offered unchanged to all cultures and times. For if theology wishes to be true to the eternal truth as it addresses the men of that time in the words of God, it must always struggle anew to transmit the eternal content of truth in the word of God in the language of the present time. The continuity essential to the transmission of the eternal truth is guaranteed by the teaching office of the Church, ultimately by the Holy Spirit bestowed on the Church, but the words themselves are not guaranteed by inspiration. The individual theologian participates helpfully in the continuity and relevance of the eternal truth insofar as he lives with the present Church and—this is his special task—inasmuch as he observes the relevant manner in which the words of Scripture and the teaching of the great theologians of the past were closely related to their time, and as he lovingly penetrates the needs and manner of expression of his own time and exerts himself to offer to this his time the eternal truth in a way which will win it for Christ.

All great theologians of the past, especially those formally declared doctors of the Church, retain their relevance for all time. But through the very manner of their relevance to their time ("*in illo tempore*"), they oblige present-day theologians by the same loyalty to eternal truth to proclaim it relevantly for men of the present time. Historical research is, accordingly, a prerequisite for relevant transmission.

The Service of Sociology of Knowledge

The sociology of knowledge[3] has demonstrated irrefutably that all concepts of human speech bear, alongside the powerful and sublime capacity to express eternally valid truth correctly, also a "mark of the times" upon themselves, an imprint of the sociological structure and of the world of thought of their time; but as a result, they possess a capacity for relevantly proclaiming the truth to just this time and it alone. If a theologian sees his task only as handing on dogmas formulated once for all and gathered into one system of concepts, his "theology" becomes a traitor to eternal truth as well as to the constantly new relevance of the word of God. To protect the unalterable content of revealed truths faithfully, the theologian must carefully pay heed to the intellectual-historical context of holy Scripture, earlier theologians, papal dogmatic statements, and conciliar decisions, and likewise he must know the precise meaning of the language of today.

---

[3] See M. Scheler, *Versuche zu einer Soziologie des Wissens*, 1924; *Die Wissensformen und die Gesellschaft*, 1926.

2. The Relevance of St. Alphonsus

St. Alphonsus's decided feeling for the needs of the hour of salvation can be seen not least in his understanding of casuistry and in his firm battle against rigorism.

Alphonsian Casuistry

The casuistry of St. Alphonsus is no idle tractate on abstract *possibilia*, no collection of outworn patent solutions for all conceivable cases, but an answer to the relevant questions which presented themselves to his priests in the confessional in missions in the kingdom of Naples.[4] When one considers with what tenacity the contemporaneous followers of the systems of the various schools defended prefabricated cases and solutions, one can to some extent judge the courage with which St. Alphonsus in part selected the most useful solutions from the various schools, in part went a completely new way. On this point the external form of his presentation of the oppositions of *probable*, *less probable*, and *equally probable* must not disappoint us. It is in the end even an indication of shrewdness that he studied the various judgments of other authors so diligently. But he asserted resolutely that for him the opinion of a number of authors—be it ever so large—was meaningless when a clear insight into the principles and into the conditions of life demanded another solution.[5]

It must be clear that it is precisely this high degree of immediate relevancy of St. Alphonsus's casuistry which forbids that we unthinkingly accept his clever solutions, for other times and

[4] The difference between an abstract, legalistic theoretical casuistry on the one side and the synthetic Alphonsian casuistry which proceeds from the prudent judgment of concrete life on the other, is correctly stressed by Domenico Capone, "La verità morale vita delle anime, L'Accademia Alfonsiana nella Facoltà teologica," in *L'Osservatore Romano*, November 10, 1960, p. 4.

[5] See *Theologia moralis*, lib. I, tract. 1, in Gaudé, number 79, volume I, pp. 58ff.

other cultures, without regard to the changed sociological, psychological, and religious conditions. His sense for concrete reality and the basic direction of his casuistry always remain immediately relevant. The eternally valid principles which were applied by Alphonsus in the solution of typical cases of conscience in his milieu obviously remain valid today, too. But often in the newness of the circumstances entirely new principles and a more comprehensive over-all view must also come into play.

We believe that we remain true to the sense of reality of St. Alphonsus today if, with the help of empirical sociology, we investigate life, which has become so various and richly differentiated, in order to arrive at a differentiated pastoral typology of casuistry corresponding to the typical conditions in various areas and among various sociological groups. If we here and there venture to go new ways in the spirit of St. Alphonsus, then it is obviously only—and here most especially do we follow in the footsteps of the saint—in closest solidarity with the efforts of the entirety of contemporary moral theologians and in complete subordination to the teaching office of the Church.

Anyone who holds fast to a narrow interpretation of a literal faithfulness could, of course, object: That is not Alphonsian, nor does it correspond to the procedure of the moralists of the past centuries; Alphonsus had, of course, applied a sense of reality to all things, but certainly not the circumstantial methods of an empirical pastoral sociology; and he restricted himself essentially to a casuistry of individual morality. To this we answer: This slavish "faithfulness" overlooks the fact that at that time society was relatively static and that, generally speaking (at least in the regions Alphonsus had in mind), it was more Christian than the individual. Therefore, on the one hand he could draw a pertinent judgment out of his rich experience of life, and on the other hand limit himself to individual morality. But we live in an uncommonly stormy, progressive, dynamic, and pluralistic society. We must admit that if we wish to be truly wise, the mere random experience of life does not suffice today. And the newness of the problem arises from a completely altered intellectual milieu. There, of course, above all the question is posed to us, just as it was to Alphonsus, whether we are faithful to the eternal truth and at the same time listen humbly to the *kairós* and use all the means given us by providence to be as just as possible to our task. Our task is primarily a deepening and relevant application of social morality and social pastoral theology: the proclamation of the royal dominion of God over all provinces of human existence and especially of the social life.

The Equiprobabilism of St. Alphonsus

In a critical hour of history in which Jansenism became an enormous danger for the entire Church and the sometimes extremely rigorous probabiliorism, which followed the defamation and ultimately the suppression of the Society of Jesus, seemed to be master of the field within the Church, Alphonsus firmly defended a temperate, modified probabilism. When one of his first and most meritorious companions in the order asked him not to continue this battle, which might lead to a dissolution of his congregation, Alphonsus made clear to him that his concern for a milder pastoral theology was so important that he must fight on to the end even at the price of endangering his foundation.[6]

What is the great theological background of this desire on the part of Alphonsus? Ultimately, it goes back to the battle led with such extreme passion by the apostle to the gentiles against an overemphasis on external laws to the damage of the law of growth, of the *élan* of Christian life. Alphonsus, in the voluminous corpus of his ascetical writings, brought about a true springtime of courageous, happy striving for holiness after the hoar

[6] See *Lettere di S. Alfonse,* Chapter III, numbers 342, 347, 402, 421; *Lettera di P. Pierpaolo Blasucci,* Archiv Generale C.SS.R., XXXII, volume II, 1.

frost of Jansenism and legalistic hardening. His mariology places the mother of mercy in the foreground, to the glorification of the common saving will of God. His work on that great means of grace, prayer, serves the same goal. Perhaps his most beautiful book, *The Love of Jesus Christ*, illumined the entire moral life of Christians by its sublime canticle of love. To love Christ in the neighbor, and indeed on principle to love him without limit, according to the measure of the overflowing gift of grace, is for Alphonsus the entire Christian morality. Even this *élan* was extremely endangered by the excessive legalistic demands upon the weak, as well as by the fixations and fascination the law causes in the good. For this reason Alphonsus took up and courageously carried through the then almost hopeless battle for moderation in interpreting the law. Today someone might boast that he would be more daring and more effective in this battle; but he must not forget that St. Alphonsus fought the first battles for a revolution on an endangered front.

The merit of St. Alphonsus is so much the greater because he had the probabiliorists themselves as teachers. If on some legal points he still seems too strong to us today, let us not forget how the battle situation looked at that time. The basic conviction of St. Alphonsus was this: Anyone who imposes on Christians legalistic burdens of great number and, besides that, of doubtful validity, and draws the legal boundaries ever more narrow, cannot expect of them that splendid work of spontaneous love, far beyond the merely legal, which the Holy Spirit with his grace wishes to draw forth. The person who strains the external law even to the point of refusing absolution on the basis of a disputed obligation, makes himself guilty of the fact that some despair completely and many others scarcely heed any longer the law of grace inscribed in the heart and spirit and give up the striving for perfection. Thus Alphonsus, in writing against the moralists then prevalent who were interested only in insisting on absolutely every conceivable and somehow probable

61

legal obligation, says: "It is an injustice to temper the observance of the divine law; it is nevertheless no lesser evil to make the yoke imposed by God more difficult for others than is just. Exaggerated legal severity which wishes to obligate men to the most difficult prescriptions obstructs the way to salvation."[7]

In the situation of that time, St. Alphonsus, through his moderate probabilism, served in the best possible manner the true respect for the formulated law and at the same time the true freedom of the children of God which coincides with the most consummate joyful loyalty to the grace of the Holy Spirit. Today, too, we must do that in a corresponding manner. This certainly does not mean that we should resolutely pursue the controversies over the so-called moral systems, which we might better call "guide rules of the conscience for the Christian venture."[8] This problem—thank God—was essentially solved by Alphonsus, and the differences of the various schools are today no longer of much consequence. It is nevertheless worth applying the principles of his solutions courageously to the problems of today.

We will give only one example: liturgy in the position of a vital renewal. Meaningless and formalistic habits—in contrast to new directions from the apostolic see—are counterbalanced by somewhat daring and overdaring attempts to vitalize the liturgy in the spirit of the Church and in line with the newest developments. Are we not acting against the spirit of St. Alphonsus when we improperly condemn "overconservative" deviations from the law in the direction of formalism more mildly than daring attempts at vitalization produced by the apostolic spirit? By this, of course, we in no way wish to recommend arbitrariness.

Freedom for the Law of the Spirit in the Life of the Christian

Beyond the question of the mere application of the rules of prudence, it is worthwhile in all moral proclamation and pastoral

---

[7] *Theol. moralis,* lib. I, tract. 1, n. 82.
[8] See B. Häring, *The Law of Christ,* volume I, pp. 227 *passim.*

theology to make very basic use of the teaching of St. Thomas that the first and primary thing in the new law is the grace of the Holy Spirit, and that the written laws, which aid in the discernment of spirits, are in a way only secondary (*"quasi secondarium"*).[9] As a result, we must watch with the greatest of care to see that the freedom of the children of God, the joyful obedience to the inner grace of the Holy Spirit and to the summons of the hour (to the *kairós*), is not stifled by a too narrow construction of the external law. The external law must serve the law written in the heart and spirit, of which it is an imperfect partial expression.

Anyone who, over-harsh in his exposition of changeable human statements, places little value on the loving guidance of a person to the "law of the Spirit of life in Christ Jesus" (Rom. 8, 2), is not true to St. Paul, nor to St. Thomas, nor to the deepest concerns of St. Alphonsus.

In this context the theories of "purely penal laws," commonly accepted at the time of St. Alphonsus, but passionately repudiated today, are of interest. Here, too, it is worthwhile to consider the historical context: in the time of absolutism the Church laws, but even more the civil laws, had grown incalculably numerous. Many were neither necessary nor even really useful for a correctly understood good. Thus they lacked an inner legal justification. In the rigorous administration of prior censorship by royal prerogative, however, it was impossible to write this in a clear and straightforward manner. So when the moralists wished to create room for the overburdened Christian conscience their manner of expression was cryptic: "There are many human laws which we cannot, of course, attack, but which nevertheless do not oblige under pain of sin [that is, in conscience]. The one thing which the common weal demands is the preparedness dispassionately to take upon oneself an eventual punishment." Are there not even today countries in which such a veiled manner

[9] *Summa theol.* I, II, q. 106, a. i and *passim;* see *The Law of Christ,* volume I, pp. 267ff.

of expression is a necessity? In a truly free society, on the other hand, we can express ourselves more unequivocally. In any case, the person who completely denies the theory of penal laws must take care that he does not, through legal bindings, cripple the conscience seeking the good.

The Pastoral Total Orientation of Alphonsian Morality

St. Alphonsus of Liguori never devised a self-sufficient theology which was concerned with mere speculation and systematization. His entire theology is pastorally determined. It attempts to serve the salvation of the soul and—according to Alphonsus the two are inseparable—the struggle for holiness. Alphonsus was no ivory-tower theorist. Like Augustine, the greatest theologian of the West, he was constantly in the forefront of pastoral care. His theology is therefore completely and entirely a service to salvation, χήεvγμα.

Of this his *Theologia moralis*, with its predominating casuistry, is only the smaller part. Again and again Alphonsus warns pastors and confessors not to overlook the more important thing beyond the office of the confessor as judge—the leading of the world to a reliance on grace and to a firm striving towards perfect love. It is, for example, most noteworthy for that time that he begins his work *Praxis confessarii* not with a chapter on the *confessarius judex*, but with emphatic warnings to the confessor as father and teacher of the good news.

His pastoral orientation corresponds to his attention to the law of growth. He does not wish excessive legal demands to be placed on converted Christians still very ill-informed and just emerging from a long estrangement from God. So he warns that one should not mislead men to opposition and finally to formal sin by obstinate imposition of demands which do indeed seem legally more certain (*tutior*) but ultimately remain unproven. Even an often heard, very probable opinion may not be urged if to these men in their weakness it will be only an occasion for formal sin. The deciding factor is progress in the good, not a legal minimalism or maximalism made into a principle.[10]

His pastoral position passed its test under fire, so to speak, in the face of the problem of "invincible ignorance." The rigoristic and unpsychological inclination of his contemporaries tended to suppose that "when the confessor explains something to someone and the latter does not immediately accept, then it is entirely his own guilt, and the confessor need not be concerned further about it." Alphonsus, on the contrary, dealt not only with the intrinsic reasons but also introduced as many authors as possible to demonstrate that there is an invincible ignorance within which an action contrary to law cannot be accounted subjectively as guilt.[11]

From this and from the law of growth he reasoned that the confessor should never inopportunely instruct on a concept soluble only with difficulty if the weak person "cannot yet bear it" here and now—always, obviously, with the general good taken into consideration. Here we have an especially pertinent lesson of Alphonsus's pastoral theology of immediate relevance for our time; for *social psychology and inquiries in the field of empirical sociology teach us with great emphasis that many who stand for a long time in their unchristian milieu under the influence of perverse collective viewpoints, cannot be dissuaded from deeply rooted errors of judgment by a mere word during the few minutes in the confessional,* even if they are otherwise well disposed for the reception of the sacrament of penance.

If with St. Alphonsus we adhere to the law of growth, we will neither confront the penitents coming out of an unchristian world with secondary moral decisions inopportunely, and especially not by the refusal of absolution, nor will we leave them hopeless in their error. Rather we will attempt to learn the pains-

---

[10] *Theologia moralis,* lib. I, tract. 1, n. 83.
[11] *Theologia moralis,* lib. I, tract. 2, cap. IV, dubium 1, in Gaudé, volume I, p. 65.

taking art of deepening their moral recognition step by step, but also the art of using all the psychological means of modern environmental pastoral care to break little by little the distorted collective viewpoint.

"In the World and Yet Not of the World"

St. Alphonsus, in a manner which corresponded to the needs of his time, offered a synthesis between the perfect law of grace and being "in the midst of a perverse world." His ascetic works, his ascetic writings, and even his *Theologia moralis,* intended principally for confessors, are expressions of a powerful conviction of faith in the superabundant mercy of God and the fullness of grace at the end of time.[12] But in his faith, along with the entire Christian tradition, he was likewise conscious that the old era still operated deeply in Christendom.[13] He knew of the tragedy of a world-estranged morality expressed by Pascal—"Teach men an angelic morality, and you breed beasts." From the time of the Montanist Tertullian until Jansenism the equilibrium of Catholic moral theology was endangered over and over by the attempts of those who were deeply convinced that the Christian is "not of the world," but did not want to face the truth, and all of its consequences, that he must nevertheless live and act "in the world" (Jn. 17, 11–14).

Especially in his path-breaking treatise on formal and material cooperation St. Alphonsus produced a contribution at that time most pertinent to the preservation of a genuine equilibrium "in the world and yet not of the world." The pluralistic society of today, in which we must act in order to Christianize it according to our abilities, presents the same problem with extreme rigor. We cannot be just to it other than in the spirit of St. Alphonsus:

[12] See *Theologia moralis,* in Gaudé, volume I, p. 156.
[13] Augustine, *The City of God,* book I, Chapter 35: *"Adhuc permixtae sunt hae duae civitates."*

first, with the determination for complete inner detachment from everything that is of the world with its "lust of the eyes, lust of the flesh, and pride of life";[14] second, with the brave realism which, even if heavy of heart, is prepared to bear the misuse of our good deeds by others for their own perverse plans as often as this suffering is necessary for our being in and acting for the kingdom of God in the world.

No reasonable person would expect St. Alphonsus to give an answer to the problems peculiar to the atomic age. But he saw and solved the questions of material cooperation in the "wicked world" so classically that his example in this, together with his clear over-all principles, demonstrates his relevance for our time.

An understandable reaction on the part of today's moral theologians to the minimalism of a too juridically expounded morality of the confessional sometimes extends even to the complete rejection of every kind of material cooperation. On this point some people attempt to appeal to one of the great cardinals of the council, Léon Suenens, who some time back in an open and courageous book on current burning marriage problems described material cooperation in any kind of Onanistic intercourse with the spouse as a "kind of moral dissimulation and a way of spiritual mediocrity."[15] Certainly, this judgment is consistent with that position which thinks only legally and egotistically of its own salvation, and at the same time in its self-centered desire wishes to derive as much pleasure as possible. But the same exterior action of cooperation looks different when it is a truly Thou-directed gift of tenderness and surrender, having the goal of leading the other step by step to a pure understanding of marital love. Surely, no experienced confessor will dispute that even purely objectively material cooperation in a marital intercourse which is deformed in one way or another is often to be con-

---

[14] *Distacco*, the paring away of everything worldly in the bad sense, is one of the basic ideas of Alphonsian spirituality.

[15] *Amour et maîtrise de soi*, Bruges, 1959, pp. 81f.

sidered perverted since just these conditions of dispensation expressed clearly by Alphonsus are not present (that, first, the contribution of the one cooperating is itself true to nature; that, second, as far as intention is concerned, the sin of the other is not assented to, but rather the intention is to prevent greater sins and spiritual dangers; and that, third, one has asked oneself whether one cannot actually help the spouse better through a decisive "No").[16] How many quarrels, how many broken marriages and finally how many divorces would be the inevitable result if we today reject the milder solution following the principles of St. Alphonsus! Similar things are true for many areas of modern life.

Catholicity in the Search for the Fullness of Truth

Alphonsus was a declared enemy of rigid attachment to a school doctrine—at that time an unusual phenomenon. In the most passionately fought dogmatic questions he went his own way, beyond all school methods. Only a complete misunderstanding could chalk this up against him as syncretism. Great theologians of our time, such as Marin-Sola, are amazed today at his genial position in the battle of grace. Even his best efforts in moral theology are due to a very conscious independence of the feuding schools. At the time when the Jesuits and their school were completely proscribed, he loved to express his sympathy for them but also his autonomy from them: "I venerate the Jesuits and the other order people, but in what concerns moral theology I follow only my own conscience."[17] His aversion to any attachment to a teaching authority of anyone besides the Holy See and the universal Church was expressed violently. "Look how the Scotist school has battled for centuries against the Thomist. In all this time we do not hear of even a single friar minor who agrees with the school doctrine

16 See *Theologia moralis*, lib. II, tract. 3, n. 59, in Gaudé, volume I, p. 355.
17 *Disputatio* from the year 1764.

of the Order of Preachers, and the reverse is just as true—no Dominican admits that anything in Scotism is valid. And yet if one of these men had become a Dominican instead of a Franciscan, would he not battle hand and foot against Scotus? And similarly, if a man had entered the Franciscan order instead of the Dominican, would he not act as if he were a declared opponent of Thomistic teaching? What rules here, passion or reason? Certainly not reason."[18]

Today, in the age of world missions and ecumenical efforts, after the solemn invitations by John XXIII and Paul VI to Christians to come home into the breadth of Catholic thought, this position of St. Alphonsus seems truly modern to us. On the other hand, this stand seemed in its own time—even if unjustly—unmodern and obsolete. Its inner freedom was and is most relevant. How do theologians who let themselves be *a priori* attached to a school doctrine, the correctness of which is not guaranteed to them by any infallible teaching office, attempt to take up the great truly catholic encounter—which affirms everything positive —with the cultures and philosophies of other continents? How can they hope to answer comprehensibly, from the midst of the eternally youthful Catholic faith, the concerns torturing the separated brethren?

If we call our institute for the education of moral theology professors for the entire world the Academia Alfonsiana, that does not mean the establishing of a school doctrine, an attachment to the letter of St. Alphonsus, but on the contrary a special holy obligation to create out of the full riches of tradition, to learn from every theological school and from every great theologian in order to be able to give an answer to the great problems of today. This Catholic breadth is the relevance of St. Alphonsus that is most incumbent on us. We are charged with it in a completely new way, however, by the hour of grace of Vatican Council II.

[18] *Dissertatio* from the year 1755, no. 49.

Synthesis and Sense of Distinction

One of the most pressing tasks of contemporary moral theology is the organic integration of casuistry into an articulated theological synthesis of all of moral theology. Has Alphonsus something to say to us in this regard? Because the *Doctor zelantissimus* was never an academic teacher, but thought and wrote as a very busy spiritual director, we must not expect of him a new systematic outline from the beginning. And yet, like few of his contemporaries, he had a decided bent for synthesis, for "the spirit of the whole." His life, his pastoral work, and even his casuistic moral theology—the latter only a small part of his collected works—had their vital center in the personal encounter with Christ and one's brother, in the theology of the perfection of Christian love. *His personal view of the holy embraces dogmatics and moral and pastoral theology within the framework of the saving mystery of the incarnate Love of God.*

Admitted that we of today wish to integrate more directly what is of lasting value in the great *Theologia moralis* into a systematic over-all view in another, new fashion—and without this new effort we could only with great difficulty enter into the real purpose of Alphonsus's casuistry—we must nevertheless not overlook a deciding fact: Alphonsus achieved this attractive unity in pastoral theology through the breadth of his theological interests, but especially through the personal synthesis of holiness. In addition, his literary creations also exhibit uncommonly fruitful beginnings of a synthesis in which love is dominant. His *The Love of Jesus Christ* is the seed of the synthesis which we today seek, a splendid commentary on the canticle of love, treating the matter according to an exegesis of Galatians 6, 2: "Bear one another's burdens, and so fulfill the law of Christ." In the *Praxis confessarii,* alongside the directions customary in that time for the *confessarius judex* and the material completeness of the confession of sins, there stand the sections, more important in the eyes of the holy doctor of the Church, on the confessor as father, teacher, and physician. The detailed sections on the introduction to prayer and guidance on the way of mystical contemplation are an expression of the chief care of the saint: it is not the duty of questioning but guidance to the "complete law of freedom," to the unwavering striving for holiness that is the more important.

It would be an anachronism to make an accusation against St. Alphonsus because he did not in his time put forward the synthesis so needed by us today of biblical, liturgical, practical, and speculative theology. He had to answer the immediately burning questions of that time and only thus could he prepare the way for us. If we think historically we must admit that the emphatic and intentional exposition of the special distinguishing quality of Christianity's moral message, which to us today in this time of a grand missionary springtime throughout the world and in the face of secular currents within what were formerly Christian cultures must seem most pressing, were at the time of St. Alphonsus not yet so palpably necessary. And even in this area, if we consider the entire life work of the saint, we must acknowledge with amazement how the veneration of the holy humanity of Christ—and in connection with it the mother of mercy—and the exposition of the personal encounter with Christ in the sacrament of love, the proclamation of love of God and neighbor found in the ascetical works written by the saint in the midst of a time so weak in faith, so rigoristic and legalistic in its thinking, introduced a powerful new consideration into the essence of the Christian life.

Alphonsus, in a way we do not deem necessary today, placed moral casuistry alongside the teaching of Christian perfection, even though subordinated to it. But in reference to this we can learn a very pertinent lesson: no systematizing of moral theology may obliterate the enormous difference between the spontaneous

71

impulse of the "law of the spirit of life" and that modest part of the Christian law which can be apprehended as an externally imposed obligation in legalistic norms and limits.

The basic law in pastoral care, to which we must educate ourselves and our fellow Christians, is the absolute and unrestricted readiness for the gracious work of the Holy Spirit. Everyone must bear fruit "according to the measure of Christ's gift" (Eph. 4, 7). This life according to the law of the spirit is nevertheless only possible if we do not, by a superfluity of legalistic demands, obscure the individuality of this most free obedience in courageous initiative. With St. Alphonsus, we are conscious that we are in need of the external law, for we are not yet at the goal but only on the way. *But the external guidance and the external law must remain within modest limits so that we may the more powerfully be directed by the inner guidance of grace.* This ability to make distinctions, which is the foundation of the time-conditioned dichotomy between the *theologia spiritualis* and the casuistic moral theology of St. Alphonsus, is an essential component of the significant relevance of this eighteenth-century doctor of the Church.

The Message of Salvation

WE like to contrast Mount Sinai as the mountain of the law to the mount of the beatitudes. On the first, one "Thou shalt!" follows another (Ex. 20); but in the second the ninefold "Blessed are you!" forms a powerful exultant fundamental accord. It must, however, not be overlooked that above the imperative "Thou shalt" of the law of Sinai there already stands the consoling fact of the covenant of love. Before God makes a demand, he refers to the saving act of his unique love: "I am the Lord your God, who brought you out of the land of Egypt, out of the house of bondage" (Ex. 20, 2).

It is not as if the Old Testament were only law and demand, and the New Testament only beatitude and a bond of love. The Old Testament, too, is above all a bond of love, of gracious election by God; and the new eternal bond of love also means law and demand. But the perfection of the new covenant is shown not least of all in the very fact that it means absolutely immeasurable good tidings, beatitude. As it was already a profound falsification of the old covenant to place law and human performance in the foreground, so too there remains nothing at all of the distinctiveness of the Christian religion if one attempts to reduce it to a mere ethics or sees in it primarily a sum of demands.

73

THE MESSAGE OF SALVATION AS BASIS
OF THE MORAL MESSAGE

The New Testament is a message of salvation, the good news of the redeemer's act of love on the cross and of the victory of the redeemer's love in the resurrection. In the first sermon passage written down for us by the evangelists, Jesus proclaims the good news of the fulfillment of salvation, of the rescuing royal dominion of God (Mk. 1, 14f.). From this follows the demand characterizing the New Testament: "Return home!" The demand is thus completely contained in the good news of the feast of the returning home; it is itself only the other side of the good news.

The beatitudes introduce the demands of the sermon on the mount. But these are not mere promises of a future superabundant payment for the fulfillment of moral demands. Anyone who says, "As Christian, as a Catholic, life is hard, but death is easy," knows nothing of the life of the true disciple of Christ and does not know the essence of the new law. Just as perfect happiness stands at the end of the Christian way, so too joy and honor, the gift of God, stand already at the beginning.

We are told this immediately by the first of the beatitudes: "Blessed are the poor in spirit, for theirs is the kingdom of heaven" (Mt. 5, 3). That is: Blessed are those who in the consciousness of their own insufficiency let themselves be endowed by God! Blessed are those who live completely from the grace of God! Theirs are the riches and joys of the kingdom of heaven!

The beatitudes say this also of those who are pure of heart (Mt. 5, 8). Man is not the initiator when God demands a pure, new heart. It is God who in conformity with the promises of his prophets gives man a feeling, loving heart. Blessed is he who lovingly agrees to the purposes of God and opens himself to the gracious love of God! Of him is it true that he will see God: not only in the next world, face to face, but even already in this in an indescribable beatific manner; the dialogue of love, the encounter with the loving God, begins here already.

The lives of the saints tell us the same thing: they were all loving creatures, and for that reason they were personifications of the ninefold beatitude of the sermon on the mount. Although it is true that in this life we must each day bear our cross behind the Lord, we should not do so joylessly and only for the sake of an eternal reward. Strength should grow in us out of the joy over the love of God we have already received.

The Commission of the Beatific Gift

Much is gained in the Christian life when one begins to consider everything as a gift of God. This means a more profound break with sin than the unbalanced fascination with prohibitions and minimal commandments. Paul discloses the essence of the sermon on the mount to us when he admonishes us: "You are not under law but under grace" (Rom. 6, 14).

Nothing is so powerful a bar to sin as the grateful knowledge of the working of God's grace. Because God has given us a new heart "through the renewal in the Holy Spirit" (Tit. 3, 5), we can and must serve him in pure hearts, in loyal love, and in honorable intention. Because through baptism with Christ we have died to sin and with him awakened to a new life (Rom. 6; Eph. 2), we can and must change into a new life.

In the sermon on the mount Christ proclaims to us his law of the kingdom; thus demands are included, too. And these are frighteningly high; hard, yes, even impossible for the natural man if he considers them merely as demands upon himself.

But the deciding factor is that the demand is not first, nor does it exist for its own sake. *It is the expression of grace.* What God demands of us is the response of love. The love with which God has first loved us and of which he makes us capable is the

75

sustaining basis of every demand. But with this, too, every challenge becomes honorable and easy. "For my yoke is easy, and my burden is light" (Mt. 11, 30).

He who has understood the good news, the greatness of the love of God, also understands the profound seriousness of decision which the kingdom of God places before us. The love of the holy God demands an absolute decision for him: "If your right eye causes you to sin, pluck it out and throw it away; it is better that you lose one of your members than that your whole body be thrown into hell" (Mt. 5, 29).

After Christ demanded of his disciples sincere kindness to the neighbor, purity of intention, uprightness of purpose, absolute truthfulness, and even love of the enemy, he summarized all this in the highest demand: "You, therefore, must be perfect, as your heavenly Father is perfect" (Mt. 5, 48). The Father in heaven, who has made his fatherly love visible to us in Christ, must be our model in his all-encompassing love. By this commandment God confers the greatest honor on man. It is the expression of how truly and actually we may call God our father. For this reason the evangelist Matthew wrote the "Our Father" within this context.

NOT A GUARDRAIL, BUT A ROAD SIGN POINTING AHEAD

But, we must still ask in the face of our weakness, is this commandment not too high for us? It is simply impossible for us to be like God in his perfection. However, it is precisely here that the characteristic of the demands of the sermon on the mount shows itself: they are not a minimal program, minimal demands for a servant. They are directions to the heights for the friend of God, for the child of God.

The divine Master does not demand that we have already attained all this. On the other hand, it is also not a nonbinding counsel. It is a true commandment of love which tells us to strive

76

honestly to put ourselves on the path towards fulfillment. The apostle to the gentiles expresses this when he says: "Not that I have already obtained this or am already perfect; but I press on to make it my own, because Christ Jesus has made me his own" (Phil. 3 ,12). In the fact that Christ has already made us his own lies a pressing obligation and a powerful stimulus to strive unswervingly towards the heights, in confidence in the Lord.

Christians are not free to choose between a life on the bottom rung of minimal commandments and prescriptions, and a life of striving towards the heights. After the ninefold "Blessed" of the sermon on the mount, after all the love which God has shown to us, after our election and sanctification in the sacraments, the Christian decidedly risks his salvation if he tries to set his course along the extreme minimal margin. He would then be like a mere servant under the law. He would stop orienting his life towards grace.

God will kindly forgive us if we in individual cases fall short of the heights of the demand. But in no case may the Christian take up a minimalism on principle. The man who wishes only to ask on every occasion, "Must I do this or that under pain of sin?", is far from the spirit of the sermon on the mount. The program of life which it demands says, "What can I repay to the Lord for all that he has given to me!" God shows us his love through the natural and supernatural gifts which he bestows upon us. Gratitude makes us quick to hear his call of grace and the call of the present hour.

In the true Christian position which orients itself more towards the gifts of grace than to the minimalistic commandments, the plea of the "Our Father" begins to realize itself: "Thy will be done on earth as it is in heaven" (Mt. 6, 10). We pray not merely that the will of God be done as completely as in heaven, but still more that *it will be fulfilled in the same manner in which the angels and saints of heaven fulfill it.* In heaven there is no longer any prohibition and no minimal laws defining the limits of sin. There everything happens as response to the love of God. Therefore, the will of God there also means purest beatitude.

The law of Christ already here on earth—the sermon on the mount tells us this—is completely and entirely good tidings. The Lord wishes to make us happy. His love wishes to capture our hearts so completely that we do good not only for the sake of eternal reward, in order to be happy in the future, but even more out of gratitude, out of the happiness already beginning for one who is beloved by God and who loves God with a pure heart.

THE ALL-INCLUSIVE MESSAGE OF THE SERMON ON THE MOUNT

The sermon on the mount leaves us no doubt that renewal proceeds from within, from the heart of man. "Blessed are the pure in heart" (Mt. 5, 8). The heart in biblical usage is the sum total of love, hope, striving—of the innermost sentiments and motives. The beatitude of the Lord applies, therefore, to pure sentiments, sincere conscience, genuine motives. Nevertheless, Jesus is not concerned in the sermon on the mount with pure inwardness. The first statements immediately after the beatitudes prevent such a misunderstanding. After the ninefold "Blessed are you!" Jesus discloses to his disciples their privileged task in the world: "You are the salt of the earth. . . . You are the light of the world. A city set on a hill cannot be hid. Nor do men light a lamp and put it under a bushel, but on a stand, and it gives light to all in the house. Let your light so shine before men, that they may see your good works and give glory to your Father who is in heaven" (Mt. 5, 13ff.).

The sincerity of interior renewal must prove itself in life, in deed. The conclusion of the sermon on the mount again stresses this truth heavily. "Every sound tree bears good fruit, but the bad tree bears evil fruit. . . . Thus you will know them by their fruits. Not every one who says to me, 'Lord, Lord,' shall enter the kingdom of heaven, but he who does the will of my Father who is in heaven" (Mt. 7, 16–21).

Jesus is also genuinely concerned that the coming of the kingdom of God be visible in the relation of men to one another and in the entire earthly order; for this reason he proclaimed the absolute indissolubility of marriage (Mt. 5, 31f.). He demands of his disciples such undefiled truthfulness that an oath would really be superfluous (Mt. 5, 33ff.). He expects of his own such a forceful inner power of love that in the midst of a world of violence they bear witness to the peacefulness of selfless love (Mt. 5, 38ff.). This love should be especially visible in their encounter with hostile men (Mt. 5, 43ff.).

Not only individuals but the community of disciples as a whole should in their relationships make visible the contours of a new world, a new relation of humanity to God and of men to one another. Does that mean that the sermon on the mount is also feasible in the earthly order?

The sermon on the mount stands counter to the expectations of the children of this world. The beatitudes and the demands of the sermon on the mount leave no opening for the expectation of an earthly paradise. Even the "Blessed are you!" which the Lord addresses to those who suffer persecution for the sake of his name forbids his disciples the naïve dream of an improving world. All beatitudes point out the way of the cross. They demand the readiness to carry hope in God and joy in his love through to the end amid earthly frustrations. Care for earthly things must recede: "But seek first his kingdom and his righteousness, and all these things shall be yours as well" (Mt. 6, 33). But "to seek the kingdom of God" does not mean to withdraw into pure inwardness and give the earthly order over to the wicked.

The sermon on the mount says nothing directly about whether earthly power is good or evil. But it forbids selfish striving after power to the disciples of Christ. It is their task to work selflessly for the dominion of God over all areas of life. "Blessed are the meek, for they shall inherit the earth" (Mt. 5, 5).

The concentrated power of patient love, of humble courage to renounce self-success, is what makes the commitment of the disciples of Christ to the all-encompassing kingdom of God credible.

All the frighteningly high demands of the sermon on the mount presuppose that the liberating strength of divine love is now already powerfully at work, but that the final condition of completion is nevertheless still not at hand. The disciple of Christ believes that Christ is the redeemer of the world and that thus a life of a disciple in conformity with grace also means salvation for the world and its order. But he must also know that this is a wicked world and that "the lust of the flesh and the lust of the eyes and the pride of life" is of the world (1 Jn. 2, 16), that indeed the battle at the end of time is still to be not only against flesh and blood but "against the world rulers of this present darkness" (Eph. 6, 12).

The disciples of Christ are not of the world, but they have a commission in the world (Jn. 17, 16ff.). They can fulfill this only if they are at the same time "as wise as serpents and innocent as doves" (Mt. 10, 16). They must also approach their worldly task "in the simplicity of doves"; we might just as well say "in the spirit of the sermon on the mount."

Neither Violence nor Fanaticism

For a believer the solution to the question "Must politics also orient itself to the sermon on the mount?" lies in the mean between two extremes. The one type, which found its literary expression in Dostoevsky's Grand Inquisitor, wishes to pursue the improvement of the world in all too human prudence. For practical purposes he does not believe in the renewal of the human heart and in the fulfillment of salvation at the end of time. Thus he seeks to enforce a better order with means which are intrinsically foreign to the sermon on the mount. He expects everything to come from a hard administration of the external law. He lacks that patience and meekness which is the fruit of Christian hope in the new heaven and the new earth which will be given to us only with the second coming of Christ. Through the sermon on the mount judgment is spoken on impatient struggles of this kind for a "more Christian" public order: only the meek, the absolutely undefiled, the simple believers will possess the land (see Mt. 5, 5).

The other extreme presents the fanatics of various stamps. They try in their way to be simple as doves. But their superficial simplicity glosses over the disturbing "folly of the cross," which is the wisdom of God, because they lack Christian prudence, the humble sense of the reality of this interval between the first and second comings of Christ. They do not reckon, or not seriously enough, with the perversion in their own breast and with the "powers of darkness" which have not yet given up their battle.

On the contrary, the fanatics believe in their imprudence that they should endure this very powerlessness and renunciation of any resistance to injustice, whereas with this attitude they actually permit, even strengthen, the forces of evil. In their guilelessness they not seldom let themselves be misused for the intrigues of the wicked. Often it is not only wisdom that they lack; the loud, self-confident manner with which they strongly recommend their ideas of powerlessness betrays the fact that they are also wanting in dove-like simplicity.

Only those who first of all pay attention to the renewal of the heart but at the same time also bear in mind the tension between the already present and active powers of the kingdom of God and the hard realities of a world not yet transfigured, a world indeed somewhat hostile to God, will approach their task in the world in the spirit of the sermon on the mount, without letting themselves at the same time be innocently misused by the wicked. Christ himself gives us the example of how one can fulfill his law and still prudently calculate the deceit and weakness of men: his person, his action, and his words are perfectly transparent; yet when questioned by the high priest under oath, he chose to strengthen the witness of his sonship of God by a solemn answer. So, too, the disciple will not be untrue to the demands of the sermon on the mount if for cogent reasons he takes an oath.

As long as breakers of law and security threaten, there remains the need of the power of threat. Too great mildness to the law-breaker becomes unkindness to those who are handed over without protection to malice, unkindness also to the weak and unstable who can be effectively discouraged from evil only by fear of punishment. As long as there are states which stir up revolt and world revolution and are restrained from armed assault only by the fear of powerful resistance, the right and the duty of self-defense remains for peace-loving peoples.

The Supremacy of the Spirit of the Sermon on the Mount

But what then remains of the sermon on the mount for public life if the Christian still champions the necessity of the oath, of the power of threat and punishment, and readiness to defend?

If he places his entire confidence in these means, there remains, in fact, nothing of the spirit of the sermon on the mount. The Christian must not believe that better laws, a sufficiently strict management of punitive force, and defense preparations alone suffice. His first concern must be that the convictions demanded by the sermon on the mount also take form in this sphere. Thus, for example, those Christians who must apply the penal law against lawbreakers will meet these unfortunate individuals with sincere kindness and with genuine well-wishing, and will not cease caring for their welfare and eternal salvation even if they experience ingratitude.

If true Christians in their responsibility demand a readiness to defend themselves, they will be especially intent to abstain from every unkind word and every disapproving judgment on foreign peoples and their ways, and to meet the individuals of a foreign country in sincere love. The Christian politician will be prepared to better the atmosphere of mutual understanding by prudent flexibility. But he will not do this only out of political calculations. Rather everything should be an expression of peaceableness, righteousness, truthfulness, and genuine love of the enemy.

Men whose being and action reflect the spirit of the sermon on the mount have much more influence in public life than penal law, penitentiaries, and armies. If at least a large proportion of Christians begin to live according to the sermon on the mount, then some of the clouds of prejudice, of hate and group egotism in the world would vanish. Were the politicians who are Christians animated always by the spirit of the sermon on the mount, then they could intercede much more effectively for justice and righteousness and serve the true interests of the people: for passion makes blind, but true love makes perceptive. Absolute fidelity and truthfulness create confidence.

Pacem in terris, the encyclical of John XXIII which addresses itself to all men of good will and applies a great many arguments which are accessible to mere reason, nevertheless gently leads again and again to the spirit and the leading ideas of the sermon on the mount. Even if we may not demand of others that perfection to which the sermon on the mount guides us, we must nevertheless individually and in common do our share that its spirit may more and more take form. This among other things is to be understood in the invitation: "Once again we admonish our sons to stand ready to contribute to and cooperate in the carrying out of public tasks, to promote the welfare of all mankind and their own political community. Likewise, they should apply themselves in the light of the faith and in the power of love so that the economic and social institutions which serve education and culture will—far from proving hindrances to men—help them to fulfill themselves in the area of the natural as well as the supernatural."[1]

In the entire area of social ethics and especially of political ethics great progress is still to be expected, especially in the synthesis of natural law and the spirit of the sermon on the mount. The pontificate of John XXIII and the Second Vatican Council will perhaps later be seen as milestones on this way. Certainly, genuine thinking on the natural law is not undermined by a clear orientation to the sermon on the mount, but rather only then gains its true dimension, that which God had destined for his creation in Christ Jesus. The Christian virtue of justice is, after all, not a competitor of a noble-spirited love of neighbor, but one of its forms of expression, as Augustine already emphasized: "Justice is that love which serves only God and thus brings into the order of salvation all else that is entrusted to man."[2]

THE INTERMEDIATE SITUATION

Does it perhaps follow from what has been said that the Christian who orients himself to the sermon on the mount does not need to take the prohibitions and the minimal commandments seriously? By no means! Precisely because he unwaveringly and happily strives towards the heights of Christian demands, he leaves the warning tablets behind him; he will even far surpass the minimal commandments.

But now the good news, our joy and gratitude for it, still do not fulfill our entire aspiration and yearning—and especially in the hours of temptation the Christian will again and again dis-

[1] *Pacem in terris,* Part V, Article 146.
[2] Augustine, *De moribus Ecclesiae catholicae,* lib. I, cap. XV; *PL* 32, p. 1322.

cover the urgency of the request: "Thy will be done on earth as it is in heaven!" In this intermediate state between the first coming of Christ and the full manifestation of his kingdom at the second coming we still are in constant need of the warning tablets, the minimal demands of the commandments which define limits. But if we believe with our whole hearts and look for the fulfillment of salvation of this time of grace, we will not let ourselves be so fascinated by the guardrail of the marginal commandment that the striving towards the heights may appear something secondary to us. It is not with confidence in himself but with hope in the power and the grace of God that the Christian believes it is possible for himself to be kind, selfless, and absolutely truthful, and even to love his enemy in such a way that he may in all this prove himself a child of the heavenly Father (Mt. 5, 45).

TIME OF RENEWAL

The Power of Renewal

MAY we and should we expect great things of the post-conciliar Church? The answer can only be a vigorous *yes.* But then, of course, we must know what our optimism is based on. The human weaknesses and even more the human obstinacy which believes that all of yesterday's traditional forms must be preserved absolutely creates difficulties for us. Each of us feels for himself how difficult it is to achieve the correct balance between loyalty to the traditional values and openness to the summons of the time. Our weaknesses and our sins affect the Church. She suffers under them and has constant struggles to overcome them, for it is not permitted her simply to write off and eliminate the weak, the lame, the formalists, the legalists. Paul fought against the too legalistic-minded Jewish Christians, but he did not eliminate them from the Church; rather he struggled for the alteration of their disposition. With untiring patience, with word and example, he preached the living good news of the powerful dominion of grace.

The Church will have to lead a tenacious battle of love against her own sons and daughters who are too legalistic minded, who are rigid, who think only of preserving the past. She will have lovingly to restrain those who plunge ahead too impatiently. It is indeed most important to preserve the bond of unity and of peace. The Church must make her way as a whole. It is no help when a little group hurries ahead boldly but thus breaks off its connection with the majority. Will she succeed in moving all to a new courageous reconstruction, to a true renewal in the spirit? We may and must expect it from the grace of God. This is the most important point in all the works of renewal in the Church: to give glory to God and to entreat all from him and thus to place an imperturbable confidence in his magnanimity.

It is God's will that the Church constantly renew herself in spirit. She may never be contented with herself. Alongside renewal and deepening in the spirit of faith and love there is required a constant effort of the Church so to adapt herself to the needs of the time that men will thus be prepared to assimilate themselves to the demands of the good news.

That the Church must adapt her legislation in the most various areas to the changed conditions was told us by John XXIII again and again and with growing urgency in the three years of preparation for the council. We must be very clear on this in this great hour of history: we cannot be concerned with mere considerations of utility, but ultimately only with loyalty to the task of our divine founder. The saving mysteries of the incarnate Word are the basic law for true adaptation and constant renewal.

THE CHURCH OF THE INCARNATE WORD

The Church must especially remain loyal to the mystery of the incarnation. The Word of the Father has descended from heaven and become a true man. He became like us in all things except sin (Rom. 8, 3; Heb. 4, 15). He became a genuine citizen of Nazareth; he lived the cultural life of his people and his time. He did not become merely a universal idea of man, but man in a completely concrete historical reality.

The Church of the incarnate Word must by virtue of her

essence not only proclaim the mystery of the incarnation, but also imitate it. St. Paul was a gifted and passionate preacher of this mystery. He lived it, for he was a Jew to the Jews and likewise a Greek to the Greeks (1 Cor. 9, 20ff.). He did not wish to be an apostle of Jewish characteristics and customs, but rather distinguished sharply between the good news and the time-conditioned Jewish laws and traditions. Only in this way was Christianity able to take on flesh and blood among the Greeks and Latins.

The sorrowful fact that in the early Middle Ages the Greeks stressed their Greek characteristics and the Latins their Latin characteristics, instead of practicing extreme self-denial in all time-conditioned things, was one of the reasons for the sad splitting of Christendom into East and West. In its *Decree on Ecumenism* the Second Vatican Council stressed that the Roman Catholic Church truly does not wish to put the Christians separated from Rome on trial. She would much rather begin to confess her errors of attitude in all humility before God and men, so that the separated Christians could admit in all humility their separation from the true Church and their own errors.[1] The imitation of the self-renunciation of Christ, who took the form of a servant and became like us, is demanded of all—without distinction.

THE CHURCH OF THE RESURRECTED

The Church of the Resurrected can and must be no museum of obsolete forms and incomprehensible formulas. That she incidentally preserves a few great museums and constantly enriches them is fitting. Nothing like a destalinization takes place in the Church; she does not burn what she used yesterday or the day before yesterday as a means of proclamation. Today the Church speaks all languages, for she proclaims the good news in all.

[1] See Chapter III, Articles 19–24.

91

That is most important. But it is also a part of her loyalty that she carefully preserve and investigate the many linguistic and cultural documents of her faith from earlier centuries. It is the immensely rich museum from the treasures of the past which witnesses to the constantly progressing life—a witness that the Church is never bound to one language, to one culture, to one expression, but remains true to herself in the rich variety.

But it is not primarily from the study of her museums and antiquities that the Church learns how rich her possibilities for expression, how inexhaustible her ability to adapt is. The Church is inexhaustible in her power of renewal through the Holy Spirit which has been bestowed upon her. The resurrected Christ, who is bound to no place and no time, acts in the Church which exists in space and in time. Thus in her very embodiment she preserves her supratemporal character, in her adaptation to all cultures she preserves her catholicity. The question of adaptation and renewal is thus above everything else an expression of faith in the resurrection of Christ and in the Holy Spirit sent to the Church by the resurrected Christ.

Faith helps us to understand the innermost meaning of the forms of piety and the ecclesiastical laws in such a way that we do not cling to mere formulas and to the externals of the law.

In believing openness to the effects of the Holy Spirit we grow out beyond any narrowness and narrow-heartedness. But we will also not be intoxicated with mere universal concepts. Every time, every people, and every culture, every community and every individual, all must in their very *yes* to the one Lord Jesus Christ and to the one Holy Spirit make real their ever present special possibilities. "All these are inspired by one and the same Spirit, who apportions to each one individually as he wills. For just as the body is one and has many members, and all the members of the body, though many, are one body, so it is with Christ. For by one Spirit we were all baptized into one body—Jews or Greeks, slaves or free—and all were made to drink of one Spirit" (1 Cor. 12, 11–13).

92

Tradition and Adaptation in Light of the Mystery of the Incarnation

THE inexpressible mystery of the incarnation of the personified Word of the Father not only means the taking on of an individual human nature by the Logos, but also at the same time his entrance into a completely concrete historical hour and a complete acceptance of all the social relationships of this particular nature. Christ is not only true man, he is also the son of Mary, a genuine Israelite. He wishes to give form to his earthly existence in a very specific and thus also a confined culture and society.

The incarnation has an all-encompassing as well as a specific social side. To attempt to ignore this would be a kind of Docetism.[1] Individuality and social relations belong indissolubly together in concrete men. That is not less true of Christ, but rather more so: he is the head of all humanity; that also means he is in a unique way related to the whole of the human community and to every single person in the social milieu. His incarnation in the virgin Mary tells us at the same time that his universal position as head of all humanity does not exclude a concrete relation to a limited milieu, but rather presupposes it.

---

[1] A heresy teaching that the material is something evil and cannot enter into union with the divine, and that for this reason the earthly, human life of Christ is only illusory (*dokeîn*=to seem).

The mystery of the incarnation of the Logos has its analogy and, to a certain extent, its correspondence and continuation in the constant "incarnation" of the Christian religion in human culture and society, in various systems of thought and forms of the ethos. These connections must be attentively considered in terms of the missionary work of the Church as well as very especially from a sociology of religion in the service of the faith. Only thus can it succeed in giving the correct theological place to the problem of adaptation and of variety in the transmission of Christian truth. Adaptation of the Church to all cultures and forms of society is not a mere question of utility, but an inner law of life. Any attempt at a merely "verbal tradition" or transmission of petrified forms is foreign to a Christianity based on the mystery of the incarnation.

In this perspective we will treat the constantly new projection of ecclesiastical structure and proclamation into changing human society (1). "Incarnation" will be treated within the perspective of the sociology of knowledge in order to illustrate from it the vitality and variety of tradition (2). Within this perspective moral theology is a special problem that is still insufficiently considered (3).

1. THE INCARNATION OF THE CHURCH IN HUMAN SOCIETY

If the Church, united with Christ, the head of all humanity, is actually and visibly present in human history and society as a true supernatural society and with a mission which is valid for every human culture and society, then it is not foreign to her nature if elements conditioned by time and place enter into her external structure and even to a certain degree also in her social organization.

The continuing process of the "incarnation" of the Church and her adjustment in the various social structures, arrangements, organizations, and cultures of the different peoples, and her

94

adaptation to changed conditions of one and the same people, in no way contradicts the absolute truth of her message and her supernatural mission. But Christ in the Church wishes to be as close to each time and each people, each social class and each culture, as he was through his incarnation in Mary to the people of Nazareth, the social class of carpenters, the social and cultural forms of the Israelite people of his century. Just as the image of man which Christ has placed before our eyes through his sublime life loses nothing of its exemplarity by his becoming a true Israelite, but moves beyond mere generalization in teaching how the human realization of existence must be relevant to and immersed in a particular time, so too the Church loses nothing of her universality and eternal truth when, following the example of the apostle to the gentiles (see 1 Cor. 9, 20ff.), she becomes Jewish to the Jews, Greek to the Greeks, Latin to the Latins, American to the Americans, European to the Europeans. She would indeed lose her universality if she were exclusively Latin, exclusively Greek, exclusively American, or exclusively European, or if she wished, for example, to be present to all peoples in time-conditioned Jewish characteristics. On the contrary, even the apostle Paul battled against the Judaizers. Although he was prepared to pay high tribute to Judaism and its special contribution to the mission to the Jews—here among other things the circumcision of Timotheus (Acts 16, 3) and his voluntary renunciation of food which the Jews widely considered "unclean" (Rom. 14) must be noted—so he would have thought it a betrayal of the universal mission of the Church to impose Jewish practices on other peoples. His readiness "to be all things to all men" presumed on the one side a complete loyalty to the proclamation of the message of salvation in adherence to the eternal truth, but at the same time demanded of him, as an Israelite, a constant readiness to shed externals and a rethinking obligated to truth, a loving empathy with foreign characteristics. Otherwise, he would not have been able to pro-

95

claim the good news to every people and race in a way accessible to each of them.

The same basic law is true for the Church in all times. Because she is the fullness ($\tau\grave{o}$ $\pi\lambda\acute{\eta}\rho\omega\mu\alpha$) of Christ, she must constantly imitate the self-renunciation of Christ in a kind of "disincarnation," in the abandonment of her past time-conditioned forms, in which she strives for a detachment from what she is used to, from the way things have been till now, in order to take on flesh and blood once again from the social and cultural elements of these peoples and times to which she wishes to proclaim and impart the power of the incarnation of Christ.

If the Judaizers had been victorious in the battle against the apostle Paul, the Church would never have become a world Church. She would, moreover, have been disloyal to the humility and self-renunciation of Christ in his incarnation, and would also have forfeited the liberating strength of a constantly serving truth and love. To the apostle to the gentiles Judaism appeared as an enslavement to an exterior mutable law instead of the surrender demanded by the new law to the power of grace and truth. The Judaizers considered God's choosing of their people a means of their exaltation; Paul saw in it their obligation to humble service to the gentile peoples.

If servants of the Church seek to enjoin particular, time-conditioned forms of their own culture and social order, or the kind of feelings and efforts proper to their own social class, on other peoples in the name of religion, or go so far as to exact their unconditional acceptance as a preliminary condition for reception into the Church or for acknowledgement of their equal status in the Church, then they are deserting the divine path of incarnation and are even in danger of destroying the faith by confusing the inalterable organization of the Church and the immutable truth with their time-conditioned ways of expression or structures. If an attempt of this sort is not the result of confusion, we are concerned either with mere inertia, with an unwillingness to shed externals, or even with a conscious misuse of religion to increase the glory or sphere of influence of one's own culture, language, or social organization. This sin is related to simony, and in its perversity and danger is not inferior to it. It contradicts not only unity in love and humility, but, as a result of ideologizing customarily used—that is, the attempt at justification with the help of truths of revelation—also unity in truth.

Paralleling this posing of the problem by theology, the empirical sociology of religion observes how the external manifestations and accommodations of the Church change according to the variation of the culture and social structures of the people in which the Church is acting, always with the purpose of discovering the interrelationships and the interactions involved: How does the essential organization of the Church affect the structure of profane society, and how far does the accidental organization of society reflect itself in the actual form of the Church? Sociology, animated by theological interests, will in its investigations, uninfluenced by apologetic goals, ask still more nuanced questions: What is at any given time conscious or spontaneous genuine missionary-incarnational adaptation? What is the expression of loyalty to the immutable essence and commission of the Church? What is unnecessary inflexibility and immobility of accidental forms of an earlier culture or another cultural sphere? Where are we dealing with attempts at adaptation which contradict the universal mission of the Church or represent an invasion of secular structures into ecclesiastical forms of life? To the sociologists, who draw their questions in part from theology, it will also be especially interesting to see how strong and how varied are the influence and radiation of the Church, her organization and her truth, upon earthly structures, each according to the degree and kind of its "incarnational" form. Thus the history of missions supplies us with examples of attempts to transmit the Western, Latin culture with its entire social style of life as a more or less inseparable part of the nature of the Christian message to peoples of completely other cultures. Has this made the spread of Christianity and the manifestation of its universality and catholicity more easy or more difficult and obscured? Or has the Church at least participated in this in order to animate the secular spheres of society, economics, and culture, and to transform it in her own spirit? The varieties of the missionary methods of the Church in the course of her history from the beginnings up to our times must be objectively established and placed in relation to the varied influences of the Church mission.

Through comparative historical and sociological studies on the reciprocal action between the socio-cultural forms of the Church and those of the surrounding secular society, a good service can also be performed for dogmatics, although the final judgment on the supernatural or natural source of a religious manifestation is the duty of dogmatics, or in some circumstances the ecclesiastical teaching office, and not of sociology. For without the courage for disinterested comparative studies, without the tireless, objective, thorough research of factual materials, one can easily fall into the danger of prematurely "dogmatizing" the situation of any given time. It is an innate requisite of theology to differentiate a) what is immutable, essential structure; b) what is a momentary, more or less successful "incarnation"; c) what is here and now an alienating petrifaction of a successful "incarnation" from an earlier time or from another cultural-historical structure; d) what is a current more or less unsuccessful attempt at adaptation or simply a sinking into the *Zeit-Ungeist;* e) what must be looked upon as a petrifaction and protraction of an adaptation which was from its beginning unfortunate.

Sociological morphology and typology do not in any way confine themselves to the religious life within the Catholic Church, but attempt (of course, without supposing that all religions are equally true or of similar worth) to draw comparisons with the different forms of adaptation in the various Christian communities and non-Christian religions. There can also be genuine adaptations in the preservation of elements of ultimate truths outside the Catholic Church, mixed, naturally, with a complete succumbing to the current environment. There is a typology which cuts across all religions. So, for example, in almost all great religions there is in the course of their history the stiffening of an originally living language into a dead liturgical language. There is in Japan and in other lands today, alongside the representatives of the Catholic Church, who tenaciously cling in any way possible to the Latin sacral language, the parallel Buddhist tendency which wishes to preserve the Old Indian (Pali) as the holy language. Within the externally similar manifestation there is a typology of motives and reasoning (for example, the bringing into prominence of the priestly class through a sacral language accessible to it alone, the conviction *"odi profanum vulgus et arceo"*[2] as regards the "laity," a kind of cultural colonialism which wishes to carry through the holy language of its own culture not as a secret language of the priestly class, but as a culture-promoting element against "barbarians," the ideologization perhaps with reference to a special efficacy [*mana*] of the holy language, to divine appointment, or to the "social unifying force" of its own sacral language, or just simply inertia in holding tight to the familiar).

Through an extended typology it can be made easier for the sociologist, and with his help for the theologian, to distinguish the all too human in the process of adaptation, or lack of adaptation, of the supernatural elements of the eternal divine truth and its incarnational power.

The *sociology of religion* investigates all spheres of life of the church and society which have anything to do with the principle of "incarnation" and "disincarnation." *Pastoral sociology* asks more particularly whether the Church is actually and effectively "present" in all spheres of life. Thus legislation and jurisdiction, custom and prescriptive law, forms of government, administra-

---

[2] Horace, *Odes* III 1, 1.

99

tion, and stewardship, liturgy, the difference between "formal" and "informal" structures all are investigated. (The formal structure of a parish, for example, is, according to Church law, the established structure in which the pastor stands at the apex of the parish; in its informal structure, however, the rectory housekeeper or a tarot-club can play the primary role; group forms of which the law says nothing can be decisive in good as in evil. Similarly clear are the differentiations between formal and informal developments in the liturgy, in which the deviations from the formal structure and their origins with reference to goals especially interest the sociologists; in this very thing the struggle between adaptation and petrifaction reveals itself.)

The proclamation of the eternal truths in ever new language to men of extremely different cultures and social levels and under the mutable influence of the *Zeitgeist* raises its own especially difficult set of questions.

2. THE INCARNATION OF ETERNAL TRUTHS AND THE SOCIOLOGY OF KNOWLEDGE

Not only the incarnational essence of Christianity but also a healthy sociology of knowledge strengthen the admonishment of St. Clement Maria Hofbauer: The eternal truth must be "proclaimed anew" to every age.

Revealed truth has its source in heaven, in the immutable realm of truth; but because truth has become flesh in a person, this question, if we are to have a correct understanding as well as provide a correct proclamation of revealed truth, becomes pressing: How far is the tradition of the truth of faith subject to the law of "incarnation" and "disincarnation" in relation to the various human systems of thought and language? That is first of all a theological question. It can nevertheless not be brought to a fundamental solution without the help of the sociology of knowledge. The theologian who is not acquainted with the correspondences of the world of ideas and, very generally, of language to the social milieu, will scarcely meet this essentially theological problem realistically enough. On the other hand, for the ultimate formulation of questions the sociology of knowledge itself needs an orientation by theology.

The innermost essence of the truth of faith may not simply be equated with a formula, for a) God does not think in human concepts and formulas, but he has become man and has given his truth human expression which is concrete in each historical age; b) the truth of faith entrusted to the Church in Christ and the Holy Spirit is more sublime and more beautiful and more abundant than the best human formulation, but in its transmission it is always dependent on the formulas of the various languages; it propagates itself, of course, not only in linguistic formulas, but likewise in the entire life of the Church and her saints; c) although the eternal truths are immutable in God, they enter life in time by the incarnation of the eternal Word and by proclamation in time. They are not devoured by this stream of time only because the life principle of tradition is the living God, the Holy Spirit. Just because the truth of faith is constantly dynamic, propelling, life-witnessing truth, it cannot be encompassed in a single formula or a single language, nor in a single, continually circumscribed system of thought. God uses the variety of languages and systems of thought as a human means for gradual development, unfolding, of revealed truth.

Besides this, the theological side of this question is thought through not primarily and not only in the encounter with modern sociology of knowledge, but also in theological self-reflection on the essence of tradition. In this context we must name J. A. Möhler,[3] J. H. Newman,[4] F. Marin-Sola,[5] and J. R. Geiselmann.[6]

[3] See J. A. Möhler, "Die Einheit in der Kirche oder das Prinzip des Katholizismus," in *Gesammelte Schriften und Aufsätze,* edited by Döllinger (1839–1840).

[4] See J. H. Newman, *Essay on the Development of Christian Doctrine.*

[5] See F. Marin-Sola, *L'Evolution homogène du dogme catholique,* Fribourg, 1924.

[6] See J. R. Geiselmann, *Eucharistielehre der Vorscholastik,* 1926; *Lebendiger Glaube aus geheiligter Uberlieferung,* 1942.

Human language is the instrument of revelation and tradition precisely insofar as it is *life* and thus encounters the supernatural truth which is life in an infinitely higher measure. There is no absolutely static or even somewhat fast-frozen language; for language is the expression not only of the unity of the human spirit, but just as much the variety of the formation of the human spirit. The entire culture of a people reflects itself in the language, but also at any given time in the particular stance of the social position of the one speaking. Because language in many ways is a reflection of the particular social structure, of the moral heights of a people, and the like, it follows that certain truths can be more easily recognized and expressed in this or that language than in another, or that certain truths find a warmer or more passionate tone of feeling than others.

The discernment of revealed truths—not the truths in themselves—depends to a certain extent on the characteristics of the language in which one thinks and expresses himself. But inversely, revelation also influences the character of language. We see that, for example, in "Bible Greek," Christian thinkers have gradually formed their language into a suitable instrument. And it is this again which interests the sociology of knowledge: either Christian thought forms the language, or the language seeks to impose its autonomy on the discernment and proclamation of Christian teaching. It normally requires a patient and long struggle before the Christian message forms for itself a suitable language, and this process is never concluded because the language is constantly in flux.

What is universally and fundamentally stated about the efficacy of the divine dominion is also true of the assimilation of elements of revelation into the different languages and in a parallel way of its development within collective human knowledge. The kingdom of God, the realm of his truth, is like the leaven which gradually leavens the entire measure of flour (Mt. 13:33). Either the living faith more and more leavens the in-

102

telligence of the elite which forms the language, and at the same time the language itself; or a language not formed by faith produces a dangerous "old leaven" which threatens to destroy the understanding of faith.[7]

Numerous theological controversies and battles of faith must also be thoroughly examined from the perspective of sociology of knowledge. The christological and trinitarian quarrels which broke out over the word and concept "person" are a classic example. There was not at first a univocal concept among the Greeks to express "being a person," which had to be thought through in its unfathomable depths by theology. Added to this, there then came the special difficulties of translating the Greek concept into Latin. Viewing the fighting between the different schools in the Catholic Church against a background of sociology of knowledge often not only moderates the sharpness and inflexibility in the argumentation, but may also crystallize more clearly the real question of truth. The same thing is true, for example, in a much greater measure of the battles of faith in the Reformation and of the subsequent sociological hardening and entrenchment of the original theological contrary positions.

The insight into the incarnational character of the transmission of faith and a similarly valid consideration by the sociology of knowledge of the individual stages of theological work is an important presupposition for a fruitful discussion between the individual currents within the Catholic Church and still more for the efforts towards the reunion of the Churches. Every individual theologian and every part of the Church must remain conscious of the limits of his own view and the special difficulties in the discernment of faith, and foresee from the beginning that theologians of other times and other cultures discern some things more adequately or at least could and can express another side

[7] What is here said in special reference to the mystery of the incarnation is discussed specifically in the treatment by V. Schurr, "Religion und Zeitgeist," in *Macht und Ohnmacht der Religion*, edited by B. Häring, pp. 317–363.

103

of the same truth more vitally. In the investigation of holy Scripture, the teachings of the Fathers, and the definitions of the councils, the socio-cultural milieu must also be investigated if one really wishes to understand again the complete original meaning. Even in the dogmas, the Church's expressly defined truths of faith, one must distinguish more than is customarily done between irrevocable dogmatic decisions and the actual existential understanding; for the dogmas are always defined in a specific situation. It must be clearly understood that it frequently will not be possible to confront the separated Christians with the precise historical situation.[8] That a teaching is defined is still not to say that the same truth could not perhaps find a still more plausible expression in another language and frame of reference. What the Church, for example, conclusively defined in the definition of the *"transsubstantiatio"* of the eucharist remains eternally immutable truth;[9] but even this immutable truth can perhaps at some time be better and more accessibly formulated and stated for Christians from another culture and another frame of reference than in Aristotelian terminology.[10]

[8] See H.-J. Schulz, "Die Höllenfahrt als 'Anastasis,'" in *ZKTh*, 81, 1959, pp. 1–66, esp. 65f.

[9] As Pius XII stresses emphatically in the encyclical *Humani generis* (nos. 14–17), in all further intellectual efforts of theology the conceptual formulations of dogmas must also be taken seriously; dogmas are not to be defined in any way except in concepts.

[10] See "Controversy on the Real Presence," in *Herder Correspondence*, December, 1965, pp. 388–392, and "Pope Paul's Encyclical on the Eucharist" (*Mysterium fidei*), in the same issue, pp. 392–395. In recent years, various theologians, particularly the Dutch, have endeavored to reinterpret such traditional terms as "real presence" and "transubstantiation," and in part to replace them by new ones. The term "real presence" was referred in particular to the personal presence of the Lord in his community, but the idea of transubstantiation was often rejected as inappropriate, on the ground that the doctrine of transubstantiation would present the presence of the Lord in terms which essentially belong to things, not persons. The new term tendered by these theologians was *"transfinalisatio"* or *"transsignificatio."* According to several of these theologians, the doctrine of transubstantiation cannot mean that our Lord descends bodily from heaven at the consecration, or that a physical or chemical transformation of bread and wine takes place. Rather the bread signifies our Lord's real self-giving. The physical reality of bread must

An understanding of the sociology of knowledge forbids that the gospel be proclaimed to a social level of quite different sensibilities without making every effort at acclimatization and translation. The priest coming from a middle-class family with a corresponding speech formation, temperament, and frame of reference, and having been trained in scholastic theology, must realize that he cannot preach to the working class without more ado if he wishes to win them to the good news and not to be misunderstood by them in important truths.

Of course, at this point many problems of priestly formation present themselves, for example the question of the language in which theology is taught. The significance of a language that is living, that is open to the present, is certainly apparent, but the need for contact with the great languages in which the Church tradition is chiefly established must also not be overlooked, particularly when one's own mother tongue is still not stamped by the Christian spirit.

3. Moral Theology as a Special Problem

The greatest efforts of the sociology of knowledge are perhaps still necessary in the area of moral theology, for it is precisely here that the existential character—the association with a definite situation—of many statements must not be overlooked if one does not wish unintentionally to put a false construction on earlier teachings coming from a completely different milieu. Moral theology—perhaps even more than dogmatics—of necessity always stands in a positive or negative confrontation with the *Zeitgeist*. The Christian ethic must incarnate itself validly again and again in the ethos of a time and the various social classes and ranks. It is obvious, for example, that such basic

---

remain even after the consecration, so that its function as sign can be fulfilled. Paul's encyclical, however, reaffirmed the traditional teaching of transubstantiation and warned against the confusion that might be caused among the faithful by the propagation of theories diverging from it.

virtues as obedience, responsibility, initiative, maturity, must in the age of modern democracy incarnate themselves much differently than perhaps in an absolutist society. Besides this, earlier statements must also be scrutinized to see whether besides the necessary "incarnation" we do not also find contamination by the *Zeitgeist.*

The history of Catholic moral theology offers more than enough material for investigation by the sociology of knowledge. A systematic consideration of the viewpoint of the sociology of knowledge could lead to a more just evaluation of earlier moral theologians and at the same time to a position detached and free from any resentment towards the immediately preceding epoch; it could likewise lead to a more fruitful meeting with earlier epochs which stand intrinsically closer to our present-day Christian existence in a pluralistic society. In these investigations we stand only at the beginning. But some lines can nevertheless be established with some certainty.

The fact that the one-sided juristic-casuistic type of moral theology, directed more at the individual act than at the intention, of the past three centuries in the Western Church—to pick out only one of the most burning problems—could almost universally prevail, has several sociological causes, both proximate and distant: the partly nominalistic strain has its beginnings in precisely that period of the late Middle Ages when the image of the absolute ruler with his legal arbitrariness prevailed. If one uses the sociology of knowledge to investigate the triumph of legal positivism in Western society, legalistic regimentation, princely grandeur extending even into Church life, and bureaucratic forms of government which developed as a result, then one will be more amazed that on the whole the Christian teaching of the essential law of love and the freedom of the children of God, of the primacy of the demands of natural law over positive statutes, remained intact in the presentation of

106

moral theology. Besides, the occasionally over-rigorously condemned moralism of a mere teaching of commandments found in the moral theology of past epochs gains a new meaning if one knows that at the time when this form of moral theology was customary, Western society still thought religiously through and through. It was at that time not so urgently necessary to stress the newness and otherness of Christian moral teaching as sharply as it is perhaps today in a secularized milieu and in the face of a pluralistic society from which that which is Christian must by conscious differentiation detach itself. Much which today in another situation seems strange or even shocking for the Christian conscience had in its day a completely different sound, indeed at times a completely different meaning, and acted as a more or less successful missionary adaptation to the spiritual style of past times.

Only the person who knows his historical background can judge a theologian justly. In this it must be seen how the moral theologian must reckon with the social situation of his time still more immediately than the dogmatician. The moral theologian not only has the moral message of the gospel at any given time to proclaim in the language and form of expression of his time; he must also take a stand immediately on the concrete moral problems; and he must give his answer, substantiated in the gospel, a motivation which speaks to the men of his own time.

The sociology of knowledge and theological evaluation of earlier theologians, especially of prominent doctors of the church, shows with inexorable clarity that theological work is always to be done anew. Only from the strength of a living faith and in closest contact with tradition and at the same time with the present life in the Church and society can an approximate "incarnation" of supratemporal truth succeed from time to time. Of course, the richer the life of the Church in a definite epoch

107

and more complete the sword of the spirit which the language and *Zeitgeist* offer, so much the more can a great theologian succeed in giving a classical presentation of Catholic truth. But it must be regarded as classic for future theology in that it was turned with all its strength towards eternal truth *and* at the same time toward its own time.

The Specter of Monopolism

EXPERIENCED specialists in the area of advertising and public relations tell us how greatly a monopolistic society differs in its conduct and its methods from other societies which live only by the good will of the buyers or customers. If a powerful society has a monopoly and accordingly need fear no competition, it easily becomes inflexible, inert, and arrogant. Because one is not oriented to the favor of the buyers, one makes no special efforts to familiarize himself with their sensitivities and their desires.

Only a naïve person could think that because a monopolistic society has no expensive advertising to sustain, it can concentrate all its strength within, attend more closely to a constantly better production and to a healthy industrial climate. This is far from correct. Because such a society does not serve those outside, does not patiently try to win respect, but rather dominates, this attitude carries over more and more to the "human relations" within its own organism. The truth about the monopolistic society will come to light clearly on that day on which it again has to reckon with a strong competition. Then it would need not only to adapt its advertising methods or to canvass the tastes and the requirements of its customers, but also to initiate a full self-analysis and restructuring within.

The task of Vatican Council II is similar in many respects

to this procedure of adapting a monopolistic society into a *serving society* which asks for love. In this comparison we remain quite conscious that the Church in her innermost being stands beyond such comparison; but in her appearances and structures there is more than an analogy.

We should draw our ultimate conclusions, therefore, from the fact that the Church was not founded to vindicate a monopoly of power, but to serve. Nothing is forbidden more by the truth of the gospel than the satisfied attitude of the monopolist. The truth of salvation can be correctly recognized and proclaimed only in great love for those whom it addresses. The Church has no cultural monopoly. The very knowledge of its divine fullness of power must make her messengers humble and awaken the readiness to acknowledge gratefully everything good outside her outward form and to further the cooperation of all men of good will. Because distant or recent epochs have nourished in the Church the temptation of monopoly, a courageous examination of conscience is necessary today.

Renunciation of Every Monopoly of Power

The Church is the only beloved bride of him who made himself the servant of all, although he is Lord of all. In himself Christ possesses the monopoly of power. In the end all knees will bend, and all must confess: "Jesus Christ is Lord" (Phil. 2, 11). But he has not come to our earth to have himself served. Neither by exterior pomp nor by indulgence of the influential currents has he sought the favor of the rich or the broad masses. He relies upon the soliciting power of his love.

This love lets him speak profoundly to the true necessities of the human heart. But in this love he does not at all wish to claim a monopoly of goodness for himself, for his human appearance. To the ruler who considers himself morally virtuous and addresses Jesus with "Good Teacher," he answers: "Why do you call me good? No one is good but God alone" (Lk. 18,

110

10). But at the same time he shows this legally blameless man the way in which he, like the Son of man, could become a reflection of the goodness of the heavenly Father: instead of boasting of his preëminence as a rich man, he should serve the poor with his possessions (Lk. 18, 22).

The apostles to whom the Master handed over all fullness of power have the same prerogatives as he himself: he, the Lord and Master, washed the feet of his own. He performed for them the most humble service and demonstrated to them the greatest love, which is prepared even to surrender life. "You also ought to wash one another's feet. . . . He who is sent is not greater than he who sent him. If you know these things, blessed are you if you do them" (Jn. 14, 15ff.).

Thus the Church does have as it were a monopoly, a unique place of privilege: she must in every respect be *the servant of all*. She cannot prove herself the Church of Christ before men if she does not surpass all other communities in power of sympathy, in love, in readiness to serve.

St. Paul proved to his libelers that he was an ambassador of Christ in that he, like the Lord, was ready to renounce all power monopoly. Had he, in a too human manner, been concerned only with making a good impression, then he would have been no servant of Christ (Gal. 1, 10). "I try to please all men in everything that I do, not seeking my own advantage, but that of many, that they may be saved. Be imitators of me, as I am of Christ" (1 Cor. 10, 33). His zeal for Christ and the salvation of men taught him to identify himself lovingly with all things and to take all things seriously in their own way, even—so far as it is possible—to adapt himself to them.

Monopoly of Truth?

The Catholic Church is, according to her understanding of herself, the only authorized proclaimer of the message of salvation. She is the trustworthy expounder of the truths of revelation.

111

What the entire Church proclaims by common teaching, or what the pope in consultation with his bishops proclaims as revealed truth in solemn binding decision, is true and remains true for all men and for all times. In this, as in the dispensing of the holy sacraments, the Church cannot consider herself as one religion alongside many others.

And yet this unique preëminence permits her at least to appear in the style of an economic monopolistic society. The Church is not mistress but *servant* of the truth. She possesses the truth only in believing obedience of God. To men she is the servant of the saving truth.

The truth, which is given by the God of love, does not tolerate being used to "hit someone over the head." The truth of salvation is no instrument of power. Only as one serves through the witness of faith and love can one hand it on.

The saving truth obliges its messengers to a patient loving solicitation for a free, willing acceptance. No one may and can be forced into accepting the faith; that follows from the nature of the message of salvation and from the nature of faith, which is a free, joyful *yes* to the conquering and redeeming truth.

Certainly, the Church must also proclaim that everyone who culpably rejects the truth remains in the darkness and forfeits salvation forever. But this can be recognizable, perceptible, and experienceable only to those who have felt the winning power of the truth in love.

Finally, it is also to be noted that the Church has no monopoly on the truth in the sense that no truth whatsoever exists outside her visible structure. On the contrary, the Church has a great respect for the "seed of the divine truth"[1]—as even the Fathers of the Church said—even among those still standing outside. The Church must esteem highly all honest strivings towards truth, no matter where they are found; for wherever someone recognizes truth, the assistance of God is at work. The Church

[1] St. Clement of Alexandria.

112

does not proclaim human reason a "whore" if it really is seeking truth. It can, of course, become a "whore," so to say, a "marriage-breaker," if it closes itself to the proclaimed faith.

Missionaries do not destroy the cultures of converted peoples, but seek to purify them and bring them along into the paternal house of the Church purified. We do not assert to our separated brethren that we have constantly and completely grasped and presented the truth of salvation in a perfect and universally satisfactory way. Behind those things which we call their errors in faith we detect genuine essential concerns which we in some cases have not taken seriously enough. In conversation with our separated brethren we will not, it is true, assert that our holy Church is no longer unequivocally "the pillar and bulwark of the truth" (1 Tim. 3, 15). But nothing prevents us from confessing with the universally venerated John XXIII that it is first of all for us to put away our "errors of conduct." In the measure that we reflect more deeply on the saving truth and give ourselves over to it lovingly, we will also gain a finer feeling for the hidden concerns of the others.

Perhaps the clearest denial of the vocabulary of the monopolist is the opening speech at the second session of the Council: "We look with reverence on the original and common religious patrimony which is preserved and in part even developed in a felicitous manner by the separated brethren. We view the efforts of those who attempt honestly to present the treasures of truth and genuine spiritual life which the same separated brethren have and to give it due honor in order to improve our relations to them with good wishes."

It is not mere politics or a supplementary method when the Second Vatican Council consciously attempts to express the truths of salvation in a manner which is comprehensible to the man of today, and, more important, is also able to serve the unity of Christendom. Rather it lies in the very essence of the truth of salvation that it must be continually formulated and

113

offered by the Church in a manner which invites all to unity in faith and love. In order to learn this, we must not only speak but also listen to the others, must enter into a loving dialogue.

Our being Catholics truthfully gives no guarantee that we always recognize best the signs of the times and the practical solutions for present difficulties. We are not compromising but preparing the way for the unique truth of salvation when, in all the many things which we do not know, we become humble and sincere conversation partners with our non-Catholic contemporaries. If we conduct ourselves in the area of public opinion —where we are concerned often with mere opinion, not with absolutely certain truths—as it were as "monopolists," then our witness of faith becomes largely unworthy of belief.

CULTURAL MONOPOLY OF THE CHURCH?

The apostles certainly did not step before the public world with pretensions of a cultural monopoly. They were concerned with the worship of the one God "in Spirit and in the truth" and with the salvation of men. But they did know that they were supposed to be "the salt of the earth," "the light of the world" (Mt. 5, 13f.). The faith which took effect in their love also had the strength to purify and re-form human culture from within. Nevertheless, Christians do not have a monopoly on culture. Being a good Catholic does not mean that one is already a good architect or a good musician. God dispenses his gifts as he pleases.

When in the dark centuries after the invasions of the barbarians the Church was forced, so to speak, into being the only bearer of culture of the West, she also defended and handed on the cultural treasures of the pre-Christian peoples. Thus even in those times in which the Church almost exclusively held the cultural formation in her hands, she did not seclude herself self-sufficiently and arrogantly.

114

Today in the age of world mission, when the cultures meet more closely and more often than they did earlier, the Church quite consciously opens herself to the values of other cultures. How could revelation effectively form itself in them if the Church did not take her dialogue with them seriously? It is part of the fundamental basis of the mission work of the Church to enter respectfully into what is positive and valuable in the religious tradition of the heathens, for all that comes finally from God—it is "the seed of the Word of God."

But if we wish to be absolutely honest we must admit that in the past this could not be seen clearly because of the human narrowness and European arrogance of even some noble missionaries. So much European, typically German, typically French or Italian "cultural matter"—sometimes "cultural trash"—was brought with revealed faith, that it seemed to the Asians or Africans that Western Christendom comes with the claim of a "cultural monopoly." Christendom was accepted, therefore, with a reserved or cold attitude such as we can observe towards the economic "monopolistic society."

Out of the historical circumstance that the clergy for a long time had to bear alone almost the entire work of formation, there also arose here and there the temptation to make certain monopolistic claims on the laity, which quite certainly were not based on the essence of the Church and the priestly mission of the clergy. The transition to a Christian culture produced by the laity was not everywhere successful. This was one of the many reasons why broad strata of the laity let themselves be estranged from the Church and then on their part wished to assert a "cultural monopoly" excluding not only the clergy but the Church herself and her message of salvation. There is, as a consequence, a quite conscious desire to suppress or completely exclude the Church as a bearer of culture. Yet the Church by virtue of her mission in this world must also care about culture to a certain degree. Her own forms of expression in the

115

proclamation of the word of God and in the celebration of the mysteries of salvation must not be "culture-free" or "cultureless." History teaches us moreover that religion has at all times practiced a powerful influence on the arts and on culture as a whole.

It betrays a weakness of the spirit of faith and of the entire religious life if Christians no longer have the strength to view all the proceedings of life in the light of faith and to imprint the mark of the Christian spirit on all their creations in the areas of culture, economics, and social community living.

BENEFICIAL CO-EXISTENCE

The fact is that there can no longer be any talk of a clerical cultural monopoly or indeed of a Christian cultural monopoly in our West. Everywhere one speaks of a "pluralistic" society and means by this the existence alongside one another of the various *Weltanschauungen*, ethics confessions, and the like. The transition from the Catholic, relatively Christian West with confessionally closed areas to the new situation was painful. Unfortunately, the change was not accomplished without completely unsuitable methods, contradicting the essence of Christian religion, which proceeded to hold on to a "monopoly" of "Catholic" or "Lutheran" or "Calvinist states" with all the characteristics of other monopolies. Today the whole world considers it outmoded when in a few Spanish-speaking countries the religious participation of non-Catholic groups is subject to restrictions, just as we are surprised that the Swedish Reichstag wished to decide in detail what the Carmelite rule would look like— if they should decide at all that such a cloister might be graciously tolerated in that country. Because the decision of faith and everything that it brings with it for the formation of life must be a free decision—and must not in any way come out of diplomatic considerations—we refuse every coercion and every

116

restriction which in any way damages or infringes upon the freedom of decision of faith.

Tolerance, Catholic understanding, is not inconstancy in the question of the truth of the faith, but a respectful, just, and loving attitude to one's fellow men—even if they are of another conviction—arising from the firmness of one's own conviction of faith. Tolerance thus understood is the base from which the propagating power of faith and love can unfold itself.

It is a beautiful ideal that men in their innermost conviction, borne along by the conviction of their fellow men and by all forms of public life, should profess the Catholic faith. In theory it is understandable that the state might wish all its subjects to be of *one* religious faith. But such an ideal contradicts the status of things here on earth, especially if one thinks he can enforce it. The time until the second coming is the time of God's forbearance, the time in which decisions mature. It is the time of confrontation, which must, however, be practiced by Christians only with the weapons of love and justice in love.

Have we always seen the temptation which lies in the essence of monopoly as it threatens to lead to indolence in the fostering of interhuman relations, purity of standards, missionary zeal? Since the Catholic Church is freed almost everywhere from the fetters of a kind of "monopoly" of "state religion," she has gained a radiant inner purity, a more amiable form, a stronger power of attraction. To speak in the language of advertising specialists, and at the same time of bridal love, she has regained her power to attract. With more patience and more love she seeks the free grateful *yes* of faith. She examines all the time-determined inner forms to see whether they are as attractive as is wished by her divine Master, who has given her the commission to make all men and all peoples disciples through the witness of love.

The Church in council has taken a stand on this difficult complex of questions with the constitution on religious freedom.

In it ancient and underlying truths of Christianity are raised anew, raised again in a new context. Here the Church is not concerned with laying claim to some kind of monopolistic place in the modern state. She may not do this because she knows herself infinitely privileged by God. And finally the faith needs no extortion, camouflaged or open, because it is a grace from God, and God is mighty to complete what he has begun.

The demand for religious freedom for every honest conscience does not in any way spring from indifferentism, nor does it encourage it. The basic supposition is the absolute striving for truth—but a striving in that love which is an essential demand of truth itself. When everyone in absolute honesty is concerned only with the recognition and propagation of the truth, then there is no religious war, no accusation, no incessant wronging of the common good. More, the best presuppositions for mutual *rapprochement* are thus created in the clearer and clearer recognition of the truth.

The Church, which has in council proclaimed the right of religious freedom for all, does not by this renounce her missionary activity. But she is obliged in a solemn way to place her entire confidence in the word of God and the gentle power of love in truth.

The modern world has become at the same time broader and narrower for the individual. No one today is imprisoned in a single form of cultural life. Radio and television make it possible, among other things, for nearly everyone to compare the multitude of cultures and of religious interpretations. From a deeper insight of faith into her own essence the Church can, in knowledge of her abundance of faith and ultimately in confidence in her divine Lord, say a complete *yes* to this situation. The pluralistic society is a great chance for her and interiorly a powerful spur to make her countenance attractive—one of the favorite ideas of John XXIII.

Of course, the present condition of "pluralistic society" also

118

has its darker sides. There are a number of groups which attempt to enforce upon this many-formed society *their* monopoly, a monopoly foreign and inimical to Christianity. It is clear to us that the Church will hold its ground in such monopolistic counter-currents most securely if she is not concerned with a self-affirmation in the manner of an earthly monopolistic society, but only with the service of love, with the radiating power of the truth and of joyous faith.

THE INDISPENSABLE EXAMINATION OF CONSCIENCE

Now, in this conciliar time, an examination of conscience in the direction we have just sketched is indispensable for all sincere Christians and especially for Catholics and Catholic institutions: Have we become conscious in all areas of the entirely new situation of the Church in the pluralistic world? If a society which is monopolistic in the economic area loses its monopoly, it will very quickly have to examine its inner structure and its advertising methods. The Church has never lived as a mere monopoly, but she has in past epochs adapted herself to the status quo of the closed, more or less Christian or Catholic state. It is necessary today, therefore, courageously to rethink many things.

Whereas now so many things occupy the attention of man, it is an essential part of the saving service of the Church that she use even the perceptions and experiences of modern propagandizing psychology in order to gain the attention of men for her saving service.

The Church of the Second Vatican Council has asked herself the pressing questions which follow from the so completely altered situation in the world of today. She cannot and must not cling to the accidental forms which she made use of yesterday and the day before in the fulfillment of her task if these forms say nothing to the man of today or even render the approach to faith more difficult for him. All adaptation is concerned with the purity of her faith and her saving service. The question of power, as it is posed by a monopolistic society of this world, must be repulsed by her with the same determination as a temptation, just as the Lord himself put Satan to flight when he offered him earthly positions of power.

The cares and problems of the official Church concern everyone. The more completely each Christian individually fulfills the vocation of service to his neighbor, the more easily will the proper adaptation in the spirit of the gospel succeed in the whole Church. It is the same—to take only one example—in religious conversation with people of another turn of mind; first of all, we must penetrate to their genuine concerns. That person who is above all or indeed at the same time concerned with being in the right and triumphing over the other, acts like a "monopolist" and not like a servant of Christ and his brethren.

This examination of conscience is particularly pertinent to scholarly moral theology and the proclamation of morality. There must be a much clearer differentiation (than has sometimes occurred in the past) of what is absolute truth, and what is the time-conditioned wording or even only a more or less probable opinion. We are therefore most concerned to bring to light the inner beauty of the Christian morality in its every part, and, of course, in a manner that appeals to the understanding of modern man who is solicited by other ethics.

TIME OF WORSHIP

The Community-Forming Power of the Liturgy

OBSERVATIONS AND PROBLEMS OF THE SOCIOLOGY OF THE LITURGY

WITHOUT doubt, every religion expresses its communal character most strongly in cult, the communal worship of God. Cult or liturgy, of course, in the first place means adoration of God. The first "sociological" question, therefore, is how broadly the cult is an expression of and help towards the community with God. But cult is nevertheless also in its very essence an expression of the community of men standing before God. Because men should experience their community most profoundly in cult, it is to be accepted as a matter of course that nothing should act so much to form community and to maintain community as communal worship. This supposition, based on realities, is repeatedly confirmed by the history of culture and religion.

The community of the family which experiences itself as a community of love before God not only in rational thought and also not only in a common faith, but also in common participation in worship, is much more stable than the family in which there no longer is any common prayer at all. The authority of the father of the family, which is founded in his "priestly" position, has an entirely different appearance from the position of

123

preëminence enforced merely by a civil law or by social custom. An authority which constantly expresses itself in worship will scarcely be attacked as long as the other cultural forces among the social elite have not already in practice withdrawn their support from this authority. What is said of the family, from a religious-history point of view perhaps the most decisive worshiping community, is in some way valid for every religious and natural community.

The Communal Character of the Sacraments in Theological Perspective

The pertinent universal statements of the history of religion and the sociology of religion are uniquely important within the area of the Catholic Church, for here the holy celebration expresses the most intimate and vital community, the community of the body of Christ. Through the celebration of the sacrifice and the sacraments the all-unifying saving solidarity of our redeemer must become effective. Everything, even the cosmos, will here be concentrated in one powerful unfathomable unity. All the sacraments, but especially the most holy eucharist as sacrifice and as sacrament, have the unity of love and life of the mystical body of Christ as their base and their goal. *The sacraments are the teaching and effective signs of the unity of the people of God for the glorification of God.* God himself powerfully makes known in them his loving will to exalt himself through the unitive power of his love in his people.

Dogmatics has always occupied itself with this essential side of the sacraments. Even moral doctrine, especially that of the Fathers, and scholarly moral theology have received their decisive orientations from this teaching. The celebration of the sacrifice and the sacraments is not only a gracious power which helps in preserving community. The sacraments are an acknowledgement of God to every community which receives its sancti-

124

fication from them; and as an acknowledgement of God which remains inscribed in our hearts they exist in the form of the new law which obliges us to community. Today's development of Catholic moral theology is again returning to the style of the Fathers, doubtless not least through the influence of the liturgical movement. But the liturgy, on the other hand, receives its full dynamic from this: It is the light and power for the complete life of the Christian.

As soon as the liturgy again understands itself with complete clarity as the law of life and the life force of the Christian, there will arise a pastoral-liturgical concern to celebrate the liturgy also in such a manner that the co-celebrating community cannot ignore the effective language of the sacrifice and the sacraments. One of the most urgent pastoral-liturgical questions in this area is whether the celebration of the sacrifice and the sacraments— and the entire liturgy as a whole, which after all is only a development of these holy mysteries—is a worthy and effective expression of the community and a call to a spirit of community. The basic liturgical orientation, the adoration of God in spirit and in truth, loses nothing thereby in strength, but rather becomes more effective; for liturgy means the adoration of God in community and through the community and in reference to the community. The "*kabôd Jachwe*" is his people (Zach. 2, 9; Is. 43, 7). God wishes to glorify himself in his people. As the "royal priesthood," as "God's own people" (1 Pet. 2, 9), we should offer our homage to God.[1]

THE SERVICE OF THE SOCIOLOGY OF RELIGION

The questions are formulated for the sociology of religion by the many-leveled mutual relationships between religion and life, ultimately from religion itself. What is not yet recognized by dogmatics, moral theology, pastoral theology, and pastoral lit-

[1] See B. Häring, *The Law of Christ,* volume I, pp. 111ff.

urgy will ordinarily also not be easily grasped by the empirical sociology of religion. The problems will probably be ignored by it. But now and then through chance observations and related basic and methodical research the empirical sociology of religion can stumble upon an association which qualified theological scholarship has hardly yet thought through in its ramifications. Pastoral sociology can be not only a very urgent examination of conscience on whether we Christians really are "the salt of the earth," whether we also put into effect in our lives what we celebrate, confess, and receive in the holy celebration; pastoral sociology, or, to be more precise, the sociology of the liturgy, can also force the pastoral-liturgical practice and to some extent even the pastoral-liturgical theory to a serious examination of conscience: Is it only the fault of the weak or wicked will of Christians that the liturgy emanates so little into life, or is it not indeed also the fault of the kind and manner of liturgical celebration? Proceeding from a few concrete observations and investigations we will attempt to outline the most important tasks of a sociology of the liturgy.

INFLUENCE OF LITURGY ON LIFE

Pastoral sociology must not limit its investigations to the purely religious life. The number and the composition of the people who attend Mass and receive the sacraments still do not say the last word on the life-force of religion, on the "fruits of the tree." Pastoral sociology asks especially: Are we Christians really here and now the "salt of the earth"? How does the celebration of the liturgy radiate into our lives? Father Joseph Fichter suggests that "the social implication of the sacraments and the liturgy" be explored. Here he is thinking especially of the comparison between the group which receives the sacraments and that group which has no contact with the liturgy. "Out of a controlled study of this kind there could be discovered in some rough way the extent to which the social implications of sacraments and liturgy are realized. It is one thing to assert that these sacred rites should have social implications; it is quite another thing to demonstrate the social effects which they have actually produced in a given parish. A realistic awareness of the facts of social life is ultimately more valuable for the progress of both religion and social science than the most masterful effort to demonstrate *a priori* that social solidarity ought to flow from certain doctrines and rituals."[2] "The social scientist expects to see no miracles, and he must always be careful to distinguish *what ought to be* from *what is*. But he also respectfully agrees that there is great wisdom in the biblical dictum: 'By their fruits you shall know them.' "[3]

We believe that investigations in the direction pointed out by Father Fichter are thoroughly desirable. Several such investigations already do lie before us—for example, those on the various positions taken toward decisive questions of family morality catalogued according to whether those questioned co-celebrate the liturgy regularly, irregularly, seldom, or never.[4]

To be sure, the influence of the liturgy is difficult to separate here from the over-all influence of religion. Furthermore, Father Fichter could really only conclude from his investigation, if it were not placed within a broader framework, how far the observed groups correspond to the motives and forces of liturgy taken as an unchanging factor. Our investigations aim more at making clear how differently sacraments and liturgy as "fulfillment of obligation" and as an animated celebration of the entire liturgy are effective in forming community. The real sociological question is not how far the individual really follows

[2] J. Fichter, *Social Relations in the Urban Parish*, Chicago, 1954, p. 209.
[3] *Ibid.*, p. 208.
[4] See B. Häring, *Ehe in dieser Zeit*, Salzburg, 1964, pp. 185–223, 376; *Macht und Ohnmacht der Religion*, pp. 386–390.

religious imperatives but how far religious proclamation and especially the celebration of worship is of itself suited to create community and to further social integration.

In this respect, two observations stand out in our pastoral-sociological investigations:

1. In the parishes in which the celebrant seeks no community contact with the congregation but is content with mere recitation of the readings and prayers and technical fulfillment of the rubrics prescribed for him, where besides more or less baroque choirs take over the "beautifying of the service" but the people do not enter into communal action, a community apostolate—as, for example, a neighborhood apostolate or a vocational apostolate —can be erected only with great difficulty. It seems to be a sociological law in Catholic spirituality that laity who do not feel themselves taken seriously in the Church and do not there experience themselves as a vital celebrating community, can only with great difficulty be won to a common apostolic contribution. Catholics who attend Sunday Mass outside their own parish be- cause there the service emphatically portrays community are more prepared to commit themselves to an apostolate than those who satisfy their Sunday obligation in their own parish church but are aware of no need for genuine co-celebration.

For this reason we may view as providential the fact that the Second Vatican Council opened the way to a full active par- ticipation of the people in the celebration of the eucharist and the sacraments with its wonderful *Constitution on the Sacred Liturgy*. Now it is a question of taking advantage of the pos- sibilities to make the faithful aware of their active role in the Church as the people of God specifically through the liturgy and its fitting celebration.

2. A second observation is still more striking:[5] the parishes which show no liturgical celebration adapted to the community, or only recently have made efforts along this line, are in their

[5] See the essay "The Significance of the Sacraments" in this volume.

128

average of births for the past ten years sometimes astonishingly far beneath the average of neighboring parishes with vital worship services which accent community. In this we are thinking not only of the difference in baptismal celebration which in the one parish never enters into the consciousness of the congregation as a communal experience while in the other it already for a long time has had a prominent place and a dignified form as a celebration of the entire parish congregation; it is obvious that such a reverence for the child of God by the community can affect the whole attitude towards the child. Nor are our investigations occupied with the influence of family communion and the parents' guidance of their children to communion at the proper time. From this, too, one could expect an immediate influence on the tendency to have children. But in none of the parishes investigated do these comparative endeavors extend back ten years. It is simple to establish the amazing fact that parishes with favorable as well as with unfavorable living conditions stand up to 50 per cent beneath the average of births of sociologically similar parishes, and that these parishes are not different in anything as much as in the celebration of worship. The parishes with the least children are those which up until recently presented no living community in the liturgy, or where no effort at all was made in this respect.

One may shake his head at this observation in the beginning and point out that eighty years ago even parishes with a complete Latin wall between the altar and the people in the nave, parishes without any liturgical vitality, showed about 40 births per 1,000 Catholics, while today even the most liturgically alive parish achieves not much more than half. What does the celebration of the liturgy—if we disregard the two approaches of baptism and family communion mentioned parenthetically above, which stress the infinite value of the child—have to do with the tendency to have children? Directly, first of all, nothing at all. But the facts must somehow be explained. We see the connection

129

like this: The parishes with more vital liturgy, in which the men also participate in great numbers and in part very actively, are in every respect religiously more alive, form a community, and therefore have greater power to withstand the unchristian currents of the time.[6] Where joy in children is still not attacked by the *Zeitgeist*, the form of the liturgical celebration plays no role worth mentioning in this regard, if we disregard the deeper lying motives for the attitude towards children.

The really astounding phenomenon of a great difference in desire for children between parishes of the same sociological area and similar sociological structure is not an isolated fact. Other characteristics which indicate a sinking into the antispirit, like the abundance of mixed marriages, of divorces, merely civil marriages, also join together in the same direction, even if they do not always appear with the same clarity, and require a very time-consuming and penetrating investigation.

The Urgency of Further Investigation

It is true that the liturgical factor, even in connection with parallel simultaneous investigations in neighboring parishes, cannot be abstracted in a distilled absolutely pure form, for the pastoral liturgical openness of the pastor, if it is genuine, will necessarily go together with a corresponding vitality in other pastoral efforts. But we believe that it would in any case be an undertaking completely unadapted to the matter to attempt to free the influence of the celebration of the liturgy as a distilled pure factor from all other influences, for the very reason that the liturgy by its inner dynamic (or by its inner lack of vitality) is essentially interwoven with the other externals of pastoral care and of religious life of a parish or a larger area. So, for example, a purely liturgical effort for beautiful community

[6] For this reason the more intelligent functionaries of the Third Reich felt a special mistrust of liturgically vital congregations.

services in the church without every effort at awakening the spirit of community and solidarity would be unnatural and ineffectual. The sacraments need as their inner source of power and as their expression of the new law of grace efforts essentially united so that their penetrating effective language in the liturgical celebration and their command of grace—the very thing that they express—may take form in life simultaneously. This, for example, is expressed by the mystagogical catechesis which was attributed to St. Cyril of Jerusalem and could serve as representative for the age of the Fathers.

In connection with the narrowly circumscribed observations and considerations of pastoral-liturgical sociology and the sociology of liturgy, there are a few more informational tasks for the sociology of the liturgy: among other things broad studies on the sociological aspects of cult language must be undertaken. For the problem of the cult language incomprehensible to the people does not appear only in the Catholic Church. The Buddhist bonzes in interior India and in Japan today still use a cult language comprehensible only to the "priestly class." The Koran may be read aloud by the Muslim only in Arabic. (Just recently, an Iranian student told us that in Iran it has been made a duty for the Muslims to say their prayers in Arabic four times a day although they pray in Iranian only once a day. It was interesting to us that when we asked whether the Iranian worshipers understood the meaning of the Arabic prayers, the pious Muslim was visibly disconcerted, but finally candidly admitted that he could not understand the sense of this law.) Many other examples could be listed here. On the other hand, the history of the liturgy shows us that the phenomenon of the cult language incomprehensible to the people has not been considered essential and necessary throughout the history of Catholicism. Dom Guéranger, one of the heralds of the modern liturgical movement and a defender of the Latin cult language, once made a very interesting comment in this regard. It was his opinion that an immediately comprehensible cult language was absolutely necessary for the Catholic Church in the time of the martyrs, but not in an age of unattacked Christianity.

Studies in the sociology of liturgy today must also consider the change in psychological preparation effected by radio and television. How far has the average radio listener developed an imperative psychological reaction simply to turn away as soon as he no longer understands the language?

Further liturgical sociology studies must busy themselves with the question of how far the individual liturgical forms of expression reflect the sociological structure and the mentality of the predominating social level at the time of their origin. From a pastoral sociological point of view, one would be better prepared to approach the investigations and considerations of how the formation of worship can keep in mind the style of the various cultural circles and likewise of the most sensitive and most important social levels of the time without endangering its universality: to be concrete, how worship can adapt itself to the Negro of The Congo and to our own industrial workers and newly arisen middle class without thereby excluding other classes. Indeed, most people no longer have any doubt that the service in a predominantly working class parish must in some things be formed differently than in a parish with a completely bourgeois congregation. Nevertheless, it is certainly still worth the effort for basic liturgical-sociological studies to stress the meaning and the context of such endeavors in a more plastic and precise manner.

All these questions are now so much the more relevant when the Second Vatican Council has so decisively opened the doors to a genuine adaptation of the liturgy. These chances, however, can be used fully only on the basis of a deep insight into the essence of the liturgy and the present psychological and cultural situation.

132

The Spirit of Technology and the Liturgy

LITURGICAL thought has arrived today at a point at which it is no longer concerned only with the vitalization of the holy celebration; men are more and more finding their way back to the early Christian way of considering the unity of our entire life from the perspective of the celebration of the saving mysteries. But here it must be made clear that the first step must be taken before the second—that as long as the holy celebration itself is not comprehensible, living, and joyous, it cannot permeate the entire life. Along with the traditional difficulties in the vitalization of the liturgy the psychological reactions of modern man must also be considered insofar as they are molded by the technological style of life.

LEGAL POSITIVISM AND A TECHNICALLY CORRECT PERFORMANCE OF THE RITES

A comparison of the liturgical instruction of the clergy in the Carolingian theological renaissance with the preparation of candidates for ordination for liturgical service in the past century would reveal a passionate love of symbol in the former. Everything that the priest did in the celebration of the sacred

133

mysteries was construed as a communicative sign of a mysterious truth or reality. On the other hand, the legal positivistic spirit of the past century taught men to ask first, if not exclusively, "What is the legal obligation?" Pious priests, participating in this *Zeitgeist* without guilt, took pains to be interiorly pious and collected in the celebration of the holy mysteries and at the same time to observe all the rubrics faithfully and exactly. That conscientious obedience is a real value is beyond discussion. But the value of the Christian virtue of obedience was reduced to outward observance. That which is typically Christian was widely lacking: the *animated* obedience, the effort to understand the real meaning of the rites prescribed. The superficial interpretation of law and obedience led to a gradual loss of the sense of the liturgical symbol.

With this predominantly rubrical education in spirituality it was hardly to be expected that the priests would make great efforts to introduce the people into the meaning of liturgical symbols and actions. Rather they were given "Mass devotions" (or just something to pray) which in no way penetrated into the saving hidden mystery of the liturgical action. One of the worst examples of this is found in the custom, still prevalent today in numerous parish churches, of conducting novena services during Mass.

The liturgical movement of our time begins at this point: it wishes the rites to be experienced again in unity with the texts as communicating signs, *as intelligible symbols of the mysterious reality which we are celebrating.* Romano Guardini's *Sacred Signs*[1] is representative of this effort. It deals with the concern classically expressed in, for example, the postcommunion of the feast of Beheading of St. John the Baptist. ". . . bring about that we fittingly reverence the mysteries of which these your splendid sacraments are the symbols."

[1] St. Louis, 1956.

134

DIFFICULTIES IN THE REAWAKENING OF THE
SENSE FOR THE LITURGICAL SYMBOL

The liturgical renewal which, in its attempts to restore the sacrifice and the sacraments once again to the center of Christian life, especially wishes to make the symbol once again communicative and immediately experienceable, is opposed by countless difficulties which are aggravated by the technological mentality of contemporary man. Even the purely legal observance of outward prescriptions in the liturgy is a way of "technologizing" actions which originally arose solely to express something meaningful and to be a liturgical expression for the praying community. The legalistic attitude towards the proto-symbols of religious reality is a technological distortion made still more coarse by a multitude of prescriptions whose meaning could no longer be recognized. Men were often satisfied with the external "technical" discharge of duty.

The too technological man is attentive only to performance and effect, instead of to the immediate meaning, the reality expressed. He is more interested in the practical result of an action than in understanding a consoling truth and resting within it. The visible sign is no longer a call to meditation for him. He is more concerned with the mastery of reality than in understanding what it has to tell us of God. Technological thinking aims more at having and possessing, at the control of a thing, than at surrender to the beautiful, the good, and the true.

Through the increasing importance of the artificial product the technological man of today has partly lost his immediate relation to the gifts of nature and, along with this, to their symbolic language. The city dweller especially no longer stands as close to the nature symbol as did the man bound to nature. Even the technologized farmer, harnessed in a technical kind of economy determined by profit and increasing output, has as a

135

result a psychological tendency to see only useful objects in the gifts of the earth. These various difficulties, which have grown acute with technological thinking, and which have made access to the liturgy difficult, must be considered individually.

PERFORMANCE AND EFFECT

The book of Genesis does not say that God "manufactured" a world. We discover nothing in the biblical report of the creation of the world which pictures a technician calculating the usefulness of his action. All is expressed personally. God speaks a creative word full of power and love. Everything that happened happened in the Word (Jn. 1, 3). The creation is a spoken and speaking reality. Man created in the image of God can surmise the inner meaning of the words of creation and from this knowledge give things their name (Gen. 2, 19). Certainly, his likeness to God is also expressed in his making the earth subject to him as he forms it (Gen. 1, 27f.). Yet only as worshiping man—when he in adoration partakes of the Sabbath rest of God —does he remain loyal to his commission in creation and protect his resemblance to God (see Gen. 2, 3). This is the cultic silence, the listening to the meaning of things, to what they tell us of God, the presupposition for a "technique" worthy of man and for a God-like creativity by man within creation. If man does not set about his earthly work in a spirit of worship, he will more and more lose the sense for immediate worship. If work has become its own end, it stands in opposition to cult, to the worship of the all-encompassing dominion of God.

Modern man, who experiences himself in relation to created things more as *homo faber* than as *homo sapiens*, can no longer understand himself so easily in his proper and deepest being as *homo orans*. The loss of man's deeper levels—by the *homo*

136

faber—also shows itself in the special attitude in which he, when he wishes to be religious, approaches the most sacred things, the sacraments and the sacrifice: he considers them primarily in the categories of τέχνη, of useful creation and success.

Connected to this prevailing technological orientation of modern man is the fact that sacramental doctrine in the sphere of moral and pastoral theology is considered especially under the categories of *result* and *duty*, in dogmatics and in proclamation primarily under the category of effect, *effectus*.[2] Obviously, it is extremely significant and scarcely even need be noted that the sacraments are intended to be effective. But it is important to know in which regard and under what categories this reality is described. It makes a great difference whether one speaks of the *signa efficacia* and in this especially emphasizes that the sacraments obtain their fruitfulness as communicating signs of God's love, or whether one almost exclusively dwells on the problem of the "physical" or moral effectiveness of the sacraments. It makes a great difference whether one constantly sees in the sacramental structures the Lord speaking to us with the powerful signs of his love and is intent on understanding what he graciously says to us and graciously-efficaciously demands of us, or whether one speaks of the efficacy of the sacraments as though everything did not depend on the personal acting God and the words of his love to which man should open himself attentively, humbly, receptively. The technological man with his basic approach of "result and effect" covers over the personal cultic categories of word, symbol, loving encounter, and loving giving of oneself. So he overlooks the "efficacy" proper to the sacraments, or perhaps better said, "their fruitfulness."

[2] Certainly, Aristotelianism and later the anti-Reformation formulation of questions played no small role in the one-sided presentation and manner of treating these questions. Presumably, there is still a series of further historical causes at work. The technological attitude has at least coarsened and hardened the disproportionate manner of treatment.

Utility instead of Gift and Countergift

Fallen man is tempted to seek and to see in all things primarily their usefulness for his purposes. Cultic man, on the other hand, sees in everything the manifestation of the loving majesty of God, the gift of divine love; consequently, the basic question of his life is, "How can I repay the Lord for all that he has given to me?" (Ps. 115, 12). In the liturgy man presents the gifts which God has given him in order thereby to state symbolically before God: "I have everything from your love and belong to you; accept from me these gifts which you have given me; accept me myself!" This is the profound symbolic meaning of sacrifice and also of vows. Through this attitude the liturgical-cultic man is able to understand the language of things. Because he presents them to God in worship he sees them completely as the gift of God's love, symbols of his eternal loving intention, and means of love.

For the man completely oriented to the technological, the deepest expression of the liturgy and the innermost attitude of worshiping man are difficult to attain. The predominant technological viewpoint heightens the inclination of fallen man to consider everything only according to its usefulness to his own purposes.

It would, of course, be wrong to seek only in the technological eros for the root cause of all the difficulties which oppose the liturgical-cultic education of man. The Enlightenment also is still in effect; in its great concern to overcome the incomprehensible formalism in the liturgy, it obstructed the true access to worship by seeing the liturgy almost exclusively from the viewpoint of its service to the moral progress of man. The first goal, adoration and thanksgiving, had to recede in favor of the second, the moral betterment of man. And precisely in this way this in itself high moral goal of man was perverted. If cult is

138

first, then the formation of life in faith and in the attitude of adoration means to be dedicated to God. God sanctifies us in cult; he lets a ray of his loving majesty fall on us. From this follows the gracious imperative: "Be holy; become holy!" Through his saving action in the sacraments God has placed us in the light of his holiness. From this results the entire formation of our life: "So you may declare the wonderful deeds of him who called you out of darkness into his marvelous light" (1 Pet. 2, 9). In this way the moral striving of Christians participates in the fullness of meaning and sublimity of worship. Moralism, on the other hand, means the separation of moral struggle from the sphere of theocentricism, salvation history, and cult.

That the moralism of the Enlightenment was able to insinuate and assert itself so very strongly in catechetics and even in the treatment of the sacraments is related at least in part to today's predominantly technological way of life.

Certainly, the liturgical efforts of the time of the Enlightenment were in individual details quite similar to the liturgical movement of today; even then, for example, the criticism of the Latin which was not understood by the people aroused efforts for a comprehensible liturgy. The ultimate motivations and goals, however, were very different. The time of the Enlightenment was especially lacking in respectful understanding of mystery; it attempted to reduce everything to rational categories. Thus the battle against the predominance of Latin in the liturgy was combined with an aversion to the symbol insofar as it pointed to a mysterious impenetrable reality which surpassed the rational and the moral idea of bettering the world. On the other hand, the battle today is more against the "mystery" of sounds incomprehensible to the people and against a lifeless formalism, in order to make straight the way to a respectful understanding for the true mystery.

139

The Attempt of Magic and Technology
to Dominate the World

Just as the efforts of the Enlightenment for a liturgy of pure reason were related to technological thought, perhaps to some people the "mysterious" quality of a completely uncomprehended symbol and of a "liturgical" language incomprehensible to the people would seem to raise an objection to the technical mentality and a dam against its penetration into worship. But this is wrong! If the symbol is no longer communicative and as a result no longer forms a unity with the comprehensible Word, then we are threatened either with the danger of the purely exterior legal performance of which we spoke above, or the still greater danger of a sinking into magic-like performances and expectations. But these are closer to the technological attitude than to religion.

Magic, as the history and phenomenology of religion show, is man's primitive attempt to place the world and its occult powers at his disposal by unsuitable means (by mysterious "forces"). In this naïve attempt at world mastery—similar to that of the technological eros—the categories of effectiveness, of usefulness to man, prevail. Also common to both is the absence of a personal I-Thou encounter.

Numerous unobtrusive surveys have proved that not a few Catholics expect a special "efficacy" from the Latin cult-language just because it is incomprehensible to them. This can be observed especially in those formalistic Christians still unaware of the fact that all the liturgical rites are attempts to proclaim and expound something in union with a liturgical language comprehensible in itself. These people have more confidence in the sacerdotal blessing (and especially in exorcism) when it is spoken in Latin than when it is understandable in the vernacular. A classic example in this regard is the statement of an otherwise intelligent lay brother. When his order celebrated the liturgy

140

of investiture and profession in the vernacular for the first time, he told of his joy that everything was now so beautiful and comprehensible, but then thoughtfully added: "But does it still work?" Several sisters of a congregation which prescribes three Latin rosaries daily for its members answered in this way the question of why they were not permitted to pray the rosary in their mother tongue: "We are told that the rosary prayed in Latin accomplishes more, even if we understand nothing."

From this, as from the technological attitude, it is a long way to the respectful listening to what an intelligible symbol together with the word tells us of the mystery, a long way to the worship of God in spirit and in truth in which both body and soul must express themselves in symbol and word in adoration of God.

URBANIZATION AND CHANGE OF SYMBOLS

Man of the technological age, especially the city dweller, no longer understands many parables of holy Scripture and many symbols of the liturgy as spontaneously and immediately as men of earlier times. When, for example, a laborer or even a highly educated city person hears the image of the good shepherd and his flock, it awakens in him scarcely an inkling or even intuitive recognition of the intimacy and confidence which united the shepherd of former times with the members of his flock, of how he loved each one and how each member was attached to him. To modern man, accustomed as he is to turning on his electric light, the liturgical symbol of light no longer evokes so immediately the warmth of the living light which consumes itself to illumine everything in the house. To the man united to nature who receives the fruits of the earth immediately from the hand of God, bread, wine, and oil as symbols of higher realities signify much more than to the urban man of today, who buys these gifts of nature ready for use among an abundance of prepared artificial foods. How, to name another example, should the common family dinner still be a communicating and consoling symbol for the sacramental table-community around the altar and for the *mensa coelestis*, the *coena vitae alternae*, when work-shifts or overtime scarcely permit the worker families to experience the quiet common family meal?

These are grave difficulties in a revitalization of liturgical piety. Should one not then search for new symbols, images experienced immediately by modern man? Up to a certain limit an adaptation of liturgical symbols to the various sensibilities of the peoples and modern man will be necessary. But even if we find appropriate symbols from the technological sphere, we must still remain conscious of the inherent danger: technological man is probably very inclined to experience all these things primarily within the categories of utility and usefulness. The central symbols of the liturgy are, moreover, fixed by divine institution. They are proto-symbols which man in all times and all places knows, at least deeply within. This concealed awareness must be rediscovered. But because the access to symbols is no longer so immediate and spontaneous for many modern men, the accompanying word, as a means of leading man to an understanding of the symbolic object and the symbolic treatment, has a still greater significance than in earlier times. Authoritative depth psychologists, especially C. G. Jung, have shown that in the deeper levels of his subconscious man still stands in a very primitive and powerful relationship to the proto-symbols.[3] In his depths, overcivilized man longs that these treasures may again be raised into his consciousness.

NO RESENTMENT AGAINST TECHNICAL SCIENCE

The amplification of the difficulties which make the entrance into the world of liturgy difficult for the "technological man" must

[3] See Josef Goldbrunner, *Individuation. A Study of the Depth Psychology of Carl Gustav Jung,* New York, 1956.

not be understood as resentment or enmity against technical science. Technology as such, and likewise a technical profession, is no obstacle to worship and to a cultic orientation of life. The danger lies primarily in an attitude which looks at the technical as the measure and goal of all things. There are things which indicate that we are standing today at a turning point. Natural science and technical science discover as they progress the limit which touches on mystery. The age of loveless technical utilitarian construction seems to be largely past. The technician and scientist more and more find their joy in using their skill to serve the beautiful, true, and good. Much in the Brussels World's Fair, for example, pointed in this direction.

Just as the technological narrowing of view makes one incapable of the liturgy, so also technical science can and should enter into the service of liturgy. Just as the manual skills of earlier times experienced perhaps their most significant challenge from sacred art, so too technology will gain if she consciously and gladly places her great potentialities in the service of the liturgy. In the creation of sacred objects, the greater the technical skill, the more easily it can be led in its forms by the spirit and the inner aims of the liturgy. Liturgy for its part must do everything to speak to men molded by modern technology.

COMPREHENSIVE EFFORTS

In the face of these difficulties which make the approach to the liturgical world difficult for modern man, the effort to revitalize the liturgy must be made on all sides. It does not suffice, for example, merely to organize and shape a community worship service from the outside. Here, too, in the celebrant himself as well as in the co-celebrating community, the danger of the "technological man" must be watched. Only if there is an incessant effort to explain the inner significance of the holy mysteries as signs of community, as the basic source of the unity

143

of God's people, and simultaneously to animate each individual expression of community with the inner significance, will the so-called "community Mass" also form the spirit of community and make the faithful experience their unity and solidarity by means of the holy signs. Proclamation of the word and formation of the worship service must be mutually related, just as the most perfectly communicative symbol possible (the symbolic action) must form a unity with the comprehensible, illustrative word. The symbolic object or action and the word belong together like body and soul.

When today, to give a very modest example, the bishops of the world have directed that priests address the benedictional greeting "The Lord be with you" to the people audibly and intelligibly and urge the people to answer in unison, this must not simply be enjoined like a new law. Rather, the meaning of the greeting and the response must be explained lovingly. But even this will not help much if the priest does not perform the accompanying gestures so that he really invites a response, or if he is already hurrying to the missal before the people can answer. The faithful must feel in the manner of the priest's greeting as well as in the acceptance of their response that this is all meant seriously.

Even the place of worship is of great significance. The Church must not be furnished merely according to the principles of utility and serviceability; it must not look like a cold and purposeful factory but must itself be an expression of the holy reality for the celebration of which it is appointed. It should itself be an adoration, a *sursum corda*, an invitation to gather around the altar.

The most serious symptom of modern technological man is the "loss of the center,"[4] the falling apart of life into a series of disparate aims. The attitude of some theology textbooks towards the liturgy witnesses to the same symptoms of disease.

[4] See H. Sedlmayr, *Verlust der Mitte,* 1948.

Thus, for example, most textbooks of moral theology of the past century placed the sacraments and the sacrifice of the Mass as an additional "sphere of duties" alongside the purely moral commandments. The preachers, to seize upon an especially famous example, taught the duties of marriage with countless individual applications, and concluded: "If all this is difficult, married people do after all have the grace of the marriage sacrament with which they can fulfill their duties." Obviously, married people go in their difficulties to the sources of salvation; but that will happen organically and profitably only if theology, proceeding from the sacramental significance of marriage, presents the entire state as holy, if the actual grace is not separated from the fullness of meaning of the sacrament. Even the duties in marriage and family life gain their Christian greatness only if they are shown as expressions of sacramental sanctification, as a gracious and honorable vocation. So it should be with the entire Christian life. The liturgy must neither stand apart from life nor enter solely as a means of grace into a more or less secularly comprehended life. It must rather, according to the words of Paul VI in the solemn proclamation of the *Constitution on the Sacred Liturgy*, because it is "the first source of the divine life imparted to us, become the first school of life." The search of the great liturgical reform for ways of expression more comprehensible to the people and for a comprehensible language have just this as a goal—to make the liturgy "a spiritual possession of the people" by learning more and more to let our entire life become a praise of God's goodness and a prayer for mercy.

Not least, the eucharist, and with it the sacraments, must be the *centrum fidei* through the manner of its celebration and through its meaningful illumination of the entire human life. *All piety and life, not only that of the priest, must find its clearly experienceable unity in the liturgy of the Church.* The celebration of the holy mysteries must be such that every Christian experiences the personal encounter with God in the saving com-

145

munity of the redeemed, and perceives in the gifts of God's grace his task of life formation. The liturgical celebration must bring ever clearer to each one's consciousness what Paul says in connection with baptism: "You are not under law but under grace" (Rom. 6, 14).

Liturgical Piety and Christian Perfection

THE Easter mystery of the death and resurrection of Christ, which we celebrate in the holy eucharist, is the greatest event of world history. It is the most powerful manifestation of the glory of God's love and the highest act of loving adoration of God by creation which has found its visible head in Christ, its redemption, and its highest response to God's love in his sacrifice. At first glance, two things become clear from this for eucharistic piety: first, God's love wished to make itself visible and to find a visible response in creation. Second, the response to the glory of God's love manifesting itself visibly is essentially and in every respect a worshiping love. Adoration of God and love have found in Christ's sacrifice their highest perfection and unity. Any theological speculation which does not do justice to this basis condemns itself from the beginning.

A Christian morality and piety which has its center in the *mysterium paschale* does not know the agonizing alternatives: either liturgical piety or a wordless, signless contemplation; either adoration of God in its place in the liturgy, or the theological virtues which are said to be centered in contemplation. For the reconciliation of opposites and for the regaining of the center of Christian life, we believe it is necessary to bring the sacramental view of the entire Christian life, of prayer, and of the theological

147

virtues more clearly into consciousness, and to secure for the virtue of worship that place in the theological system which actually belongs to it in the life of the Church.

SACRAMENTAL VIEW OF THE ENTIRE CHRISTIAN LIFE

In his plan of wisdom, incomprehensible to us men, God wished to make his love experienceable and perceptible in a visible creation. In his consubstantial Word he created the world. Everything has come into being through the Word of the Father. Thus in the visible creation we hear the Word of the invisible God. But what is most overwhelming is that the eternal consubstantial Word of the Father wished to become personally visible and audible to men. The part of the divine plan of salvation most incomprehensible to Greek spiritualistic thought was the incarnation of the eternal Word. "And the Word became flesh . . . we have *beheld* his glory" (Jn. 1, 14). "And we have seen and testify that the Father has sent his Son as the Saviour of the world" (1 Jn. 4, 14). "That which was from the beginning, which we have heard, which we have seen with our eyes, which we have looked upon and touched with our hands, concerning the word of life . . . we proclaim also to you, so that you may have fellowship with us; and our fellowship is with the Father and with his Son Jesus Christ. And we are writing this that our joy may be complete" (1 Jn. 1, 1–2. 4).

Christ, the visible witness of the Father's love, willed that even after his ascension his love would be visible and experienceable in the mystery of the Church. The Church is a visible sign of the enduring love of Christ in the world. In its very visibility and experienceability the Church is the proto-sacrament, an effective, delivering sign of Christ's love which brings home all and unites all with itself, just as Christ himself, in his visible sacrifice and in the visibility of his resurrection as the incarnate One, is

148

simply the proto-sacrament, the delivering sign of the Father's love.

The eucharistic sacrifice and the sacraments continue making the love of God visible and indeed making it visible in the community of love. The most eminent fruit of the eucharist—in scholastic terms *res (et sacramentum) eucharistiae*—is the growing unity and love of the people of God. Thus the Lord prayed in the upper room: "The glory which thou hast given me I have given to them, that they may be one even as we are one, I in them and thou in me, that they may become perfectly one, so that the world may know that thou hast sent me and hast loved them even as thou hast loved me" (Jn. 17, 22ff.).

God does not glorify his name by loving men in secret. The salvation work of God is rather a manifestation of his loving majesty. *In the celebration of the sacraments and in a life proceeding from their grace and their mandate, God's love and the response of the redeemed should be visible, experienceable.* The faith of man in the decisive mystery of salvation—that the Father has sent us his only-begotten Son as redeemer in the visible form of flesh—depends decisively on whether the love received in Christ becomes visible in the celebration of the sacraments, especially in the eucharist, and receives its witnessing character in a life in conformity with this grace and this mandate. The Christian worshiping community and the community of love originating in it are both essentially oriented to visibility and experienceability.

God wishes that we see with our eyes in the sacramental sign and hear and experience with our ears in the sacramental words the love he has shown to us. It is an essential part of the concrete economy of salvation that we should not experience in our hearts what love the Father has rendered us without the visible signs of the sacrament—such love that we are called and are become children of God in his well-beloved Son. It is this initial visibility

149

of our experience of faith in the sacramental celebration and in a visible life from its gracious mandate that directs our life towards the full manifestation of our salvation. Certainly, in comparison to the great day of the Lord on which the new heaven and the new earth will be revealed in full vision it can be said of the sacramental visibility and the perceptible visible community of love of this time of salvation: "It does not yet appear what we shall be, but we know that when he appears we shall be like him, for we shall see him as he is" (1 Jn. 3, 1–3). But ultimately faith and our hope in the full manifestation of the glory and love of God are sustained by the initial manifestation of the kingdom of God in the incarnation of Jesus Christ, in the Easter mystery, and in the Church and her sacraments.

The goal of the entire salvation history is the Parousia of the Lord, in which the loving majesty of God and his anointed One becomes fully manifest. As beings made up of body and soul we do not await only an invisible beatitude. Beatitude understood in the Christian sense is the shining loving majesty of God in full resplendence within us. And this the reflection of God's majesty in our body is not something accidental, secondary. Grace is the seed of glory. Thus grace urges us forward to manifest the love received in the loving community in the temporal world and ultimately in the blessed community of God's love in all eternity. For this reason, an eschatological orientation is an essential part of any sacramental system which takes the realism of the visible sign and the audible word very seriously: from what has already begun to become visible and experienceable we strive for the full manifestation of the love of the Father in the majesty of the Son and of his bride, the Church. "And every one who thus hopes in him purifies himself as he is pure" (1 Jn. 3, 3).

The strong emphasis on the visibility of the Church and the experience of divine truth and love in the visible and audible sacraments is essential to the discernment of spirits: "Test the

150

spirits to see whether they are of God. . . . By this you know the Spirit of God: every spirit which confesses that Jesus Christ has come in the flesh is of God" (1 Jn. 4, 1–3). This emphasis on visibility is nevertheless right only if the "mystery" character of the Church and her message is not dissolved. Visibility must not therefore be consumed in administrative and juridical forms.

SACRAMENT AND PRAYER

Only the worshiping man has entrance to the greatest mysteries of human existence. Only the man who listens reverently, who receives humbly, is open to the grace that comes to him in the sacrament. But even more basic is another consequence: it is the sacraments primarily which tell us what Christian prayer in itself really is. To pray means to approach God. We can do this in the Christian supernatural way only because in the sacrament God comes towards us and gives us certainty of the experience of faith by means of the visible sign and the audible word, through his visible Church and her faith: "I am your salvation." We can hallow the name of God because God glorifies and hallows his name, his love within us in the sacraments. The character of Christian prayer, especially its highest form, mystical prayer, is misunderstood if liturgy and contemplation are torn asunder and merely placed alongside one another or even opposed to one another.[1]

Only the man who knows how to listen to what God says to us in the holy sacraments gives in his prayer and in his life the

---

[1] L. Bouyer in his review of Jacques and Raïssa Maritain's *Liturgy and Contemplation* asks with justified amazement: "Why do even they speak of the contemplative life as if it were completely extraneous to the genuine liturgical life, instead of seeing that it is there it has its source? . . . Is it not more urgent to demonstrate how this mysticism, far from wishing to usurp the position of the liturgy, can normally only grow out of a thriving real understanding of Christ's saving mystery, which is the soul of the liturgy, out of an understanding by virtue of faith which manifests itself in love?" *Vie spirituelle*, 1960, p. 409.

response which corresponds to the word directed to us: *normally,* the proper union of sign and word to the sacrament should, through the correct celebration of the sacraments and obviously in union with the homily interpreting this word, lead us ever more deeply to the saving mystery of Christ, by whom all our prayer, contemplation, and our entire Christian life is sustained. It is absolutely inadmissible to assert a superiority of contemplation over the celebration of the liturgy;[2] for contemplation, too, must preserve the uniqueness of Christian existence as the response to the personal word of God directed to us in the sacrament. Christian contemplation is ultimately the silent submersion into the riches of the saving mystery which has happened to us visibly in the sacrifice and the sacraments.

Can one perhaps affirm a certain superiority of contemplation because it is wordless and signless, while the sacraments are the word of God in human language and transitory signs and an audible response of a visible human community? Such an attempt would not merely show a tendency towards spiritualism but would also contradict the entire Christian economy of salvation, the visible incarnation and the visible continuation of the work of salvation in the Church and in the sacraments, the visible manifestation of God's majesty in creation, in the work of salvation and finally in the Parousia. Contemplation in the Christian sense can remain healthy only by its essential orientation to liturgical piety. In this, of course, it should also be stressed that genuine liturgical piety again and again leads to contemplation and requires contemplative, interior men, men seized by mystery.

Personal Prayer and Prayer in Community

The sacraments tell us that every one of us is personally called by name by the gracious word of God going forth to him. The apostle to the gentiles called Christians by the expressive name

---

[2] As, unfortunately, in J. Maritain, "Liturgy and Contemplation," in *Spiritual Life,* 1959, p. 120.

κλησοί, the called. In liturgical piety we are always conscious anew that we are so very personally called and chosen only in respect to the *ecclesia,* the first-called, the Church unified by the call of the divine bridegroom. This basic relation is expressed in the celebration of the sacraments in a way that speaks to our senses and inscribes itself more and more deeply in our heart and soul so that even in the silent cell we are conscious of our saving solidarity in Christ and of the Church as the presupposition of our very name of Christian.[3] If one does not wish to compare incomparables (defective liturgy and perfect contemplation) with one another, then one must indeed doubtless concede that union with Christ and the mystical body of Christ is not less confirmed in the liturgical celebration than in quiet contemplation, but rather that it is more clearly expressed there.

THE SACRAMENTAL VIEW OF THE THEOLOGICAL VIRTUES

It is theologically impossible to assign the application of the theological virtues specifically to wordless signless contemplation,

[3] Considering the foundation of Christian prayer in the sacraments of the Church, it seems strange for Maritain to write (pp. 99f.): "Never is a man more a member, and more perfectly a member, of the Church than when, *Clauso ostio* and alone with Him whom he loves, he is united to God." Maritain's idea that the celebration of the liturgy is an inferior practice of the theological virtue and even unites the worshiper less with Christ and the mystical body than solitary contemplation has several clear related presuppositions: unconsciously, he sees the liturgy as a mere formality and even as an obstacle to contemplation, a mere attention to rubrics and the like (see pp. 100ff.). The addition of exterior communal forms seems to him to lessen the worth or prayer: "The office chanted in common is of less importance than the solitary dialogue" (p. 131). In his concern for an ascetical-mystical way independent of sacramental-liturgical piety, Maritain simply asserts of the liturgy, not to mention "the pseudo-liturgical excesses: Participation in liturgical life is neither the only way nor the indispensable way toward contemplation." Here we come dangerously close to the attitude widely prevalent today of seeing in the commandment to participate in the celebration of holy Mass each Sunday an arbitrary order of the Church instead of the visible center of the life to which we are already essentially oriented through baptism. An excellent and clear answer to these distorted concepts of Maritain can be found in B. Bro, O.P., "Peut-on se passer de la liturgie? Prière privée et commune," in *Vie spirituelle,* 1960, pp. 5–32.

153

and then to place contemplation in the quiet cell above the celebration of the saving mysteries. The theological virtues are to be understood as sacramental and communitarian as well as personal-dialogical.

Sacrament and faith belong indissolubly together. Thomas Aquinas stresses: *Salvamur per fidem Christi nati et passi; sunt autem sacramenta quaedam signa protestantia fidem qua justificatur homo.*[4]

Scholarly exegesis of the past decades has shown with great care how in the New Testament two series of assertions—one of which emphasizes redemption through faith and the other salvation through the sacraments—are not simply juxtaposed or even opposed to one another, but form a wonderful unity. In the sacrament of faith God assures us of his vital desire for our salvation; in faith—in the devout celebration of the sacraments and in a life lived in their grace and their mandate—we affirm our consent to the grace coming to us in the word of salvation.[5]

In the sacraments, especially in the sacraments of baptism and the eucharist, the Church celebrates her faith in the saving mysteries and kindles in us the fire of faith. The faith of the individual lives essentially from the witness of the faith of the Church in a vital community, strong in faith. At the celebration of holy baptism the Church asks the candidate what he awaits from her. He answers: "Faith." The person who is gratefully aware how much his personal faith is also supported by the power of faith of the Christian community in the celebration of the holy sacraments, and that at base his faith is the fruit of the

---

[4] *Summa theol.* II, q. 61, a. 4; see J. Gaillard, O.S.B., "Les sacrements de la foi," in *Rev. Thomiste,* 59, 1959, pp. 5–31, 270–309.

[5] The problem is easily resolved if we distinguish between the two main lines of Johannine theology, which are those of giving and receiving. By giving is meant all the providential dispositions by which the spirit is bestowed on the world, and includes the mysteries of the incarnation and the redemption and their sacramental prolongation. But in the face of such giving man still has to make his own decision. He has to believe in the giver before he can accept the gift. (See F. M. Braun, O.P., "La vie d'en haut," in *Revue des Sciences Philosophiques et Théologiques,* 40, 1956, p. 19.)

fullness of faith of the Church celebrated in the sacraments, will for his part, most intimately urged by his faith, gratefully witness to this faith not only in silent contemplation, but also in a living co-celebration of the holy sacraments and in a life lived in their grace and in their mandate. Co-celebrating the liturgy (the sacraments and the holy sacrifice) means essentially an openness of faith and *redonatio fidei*. The faith of the Christian lives more essentially from the celebration of the sacraments of faith than from silent contemplation. But the power of faith that we experience in the liturgy demands a manner of celebration which penetrates the heart and continues to operate in meditation and contemplation.

"So faith comes from what is heard, and what is heard comes by the preaching of Christ" (Rom. 10, 17). The *kerygma fidei*, however, has its center in the saving mysteries which we celebrate in the sacraments. Therefore, liturgy is very essentially an act of faith, listening, response.

If the theological virtue of hope attains its highest level of intensity in contemplation, the one who hopes must nevertheless continually remain conscious that it is in the sacrament that he receives the assurance and the pledge of the divine redeemer: *Salus populi ego sum.* And because we on this pilgrimage of life have not yet tranquilly arrived at the goal, but only strive towards it as men seized by Christ, the eschatological orientation, our hope, must be constantly inflamed anew by the great hope-awakening signs, the sacraments. In the correctly celebrated liturgy the faithful will be conscious that their salvation depends on the manifestation of the loving majesty and on their own readiness to glorify God. Just as it is inhuman to contrive a "pure cult" which would abstract from the salvation of the soul (from the theological virtue of hope), it would also be wrong to misplace the theological virtue of hope primarily in invisible contemplation and to wish to detach it from worship of God (from the virtue of religion and from the sacramental liturgical basis).

In the liturgy the worshiping community, in the commemoration of Christ's saving death, is most strongly oriented to the hopeful expectation of the second coming of Christ: "For as often as you eat this bread and drink the cup, you proclaim the Lord's death until he comes" (1 Cor. 11, 26).

The celebration of the liturgy is also the proper expression of the theological virtue of love in the temporal world. The sacraments are the wedding gift of Christ to his bride, the Church. In the liturgy the Church experiences herself as the beloved bride of the Lord and is completely intent on returning all her love to her Lord in worship. Here every believer in union with the Church knows himself immediately affected by the all-uniting love of the Lord and included in the response of the Church. All genuine contemplation, like every affirmation of divine love in deed and in suffering, takes as its point of departure the celebration of the sacraments, especially the eucharist. "How can I repay the Lord for all that he has given me?" It is significant that Thomas Aquinas placed his entire discussion of the virtue of worship in the light of this verse from Psalm 115.[6] In the scholastic terminology the *res* (*et sacramentum*) of baptism, of the eucharist and penance, is the harmonious love of the people of God. According to this, the sacraments signify and effect above all else the unifying love of the Lord which both gives and demands harmonious love. In the upper room in the most intimate connection with the eucharist, Christ proclaimed his new commandment: "A new commandment I give to you, that you love one another; even as I have loved you, that you also love one another" (Jn. 13, 34; 15, 12).[7]

Through the grace of the sacraments God inscribes the new law in our heart (Jer. 31, 31; Heb. 8, 10). But it would be false

[6] *Summa theol.* II, ii, q. 80, a. 1.

[7] It is surprising that Maritain, citing the Old Testament, emphasizes that the great commandment of love was not given in the plural, but in the singular. What is decisive for us is the form in which the Lord gives his new commandment. It is essentially to be seen in the plural, in the community of love. See Maritain, p. 125.

to place the inner reality of grace in even only slight opposition to the external signifying power of the sacrament. The exterior celebration of the sacraments (the liturgy) and their inner power and their commission belong essentially together, just as the external law and the inner law of grace form an indissoluble unity.

The community of love experienced in the liturgy and realized in life by the grace of the sacraments is the seed of beatitude, which is to be understood as the community of love in the splendor of the glory of God's love.

THE PLACE OF THE VIRTUE OF RELIGION IN THE CHRISTIAN LIFE

The virtue of religion is not a secondary, less important virtue alongside the theological virtues, much less their competitor. Rather it forms an indissoluble unity with them. The question whether it is to be counted among the theological virtues as an essential part or among the moral virtues is not yet decided in theological discussion.

For Aristotle everything is said when he subordinates worship as a part of the cardinal virtue of justice, although a part which fulfills the concept of justice less precisely.[8] The Greek philosopher had no intimation of the condescension of the loving majesty of God manifesting itself in Christ and of the sacrifice of Christ as the center of world and salvation history. Of course, Thomas Aquinas—and in this he was justified by the temporal kerygmatic reasons of his time—took over the Aristotelian schema in the external arrangement of his ethic. But, and in this he shows himself the great theologian, in the execution he reproduced tradition in classical clarity. The virtue of religion is for him not only "the most eminent among all moral virtues,"[9] but for this reason also the animating form of all virtues: *Religio*

[8] See Aristotle, *Nichomachean Ethics* E 1129, b. 27ff.
[9] *Summa theol.* II, ii, q. 81, a. 6.

157

imperat omnibus aliis virtutibus.[10] This is true even of the theological virtues. Faith is genuine only if it is humble faith, glorifying God's veracity and will to reveal. The hope of the Christian —and specifically the very prayer of petition as the characteristic expression of Christian hope—is essentially praise of the goodness and fidelity of God. The love of the creature for the heavenly Father who in pure condescension has elevated him to be his own child can be genuine only if it is worshiping love. When it rejoices, "Abba!" it never forgets, "who art in heaven." Its first concern always remains: "Hallowed be thy name." All Christians are agreed that the highest goal of creation and the highest vocation of man is the glory of God. And religion effectively orients us to this goal: *Omnia, secundam quod in gloriam Dei fiunt, pertinent ad religionem, non quasi elicientem, sed quasi imperantem.*[11]

If religion is to be the soul and form of all other virtues, then it must also be expressly fostered; and this happens nowhere better than in the dignified co-celebration of the liturgy, in which God himself manifests his loving majesty to us.

Maritain correctly emphasizes that in the face of the alienation of the modern world a high esteem for contemplation is especially urgent.[12] But still more basic for every time and for our time especially is the sense for cult, for adoration. Paul sees in the refusal of praise and thanksgiving to God the root of all sin and the entire degeneration of mankind (Rom. 1, 21–32). The basic evil of our time is the profanation of human existence and secularization in morality. The liturgical movement is, as Pius XII repeatedly emphasized, a gift of God to our time. Christians molded by liturgical piety do not see everything primarily in the perspective of their own perfection, but first as the glorification of God. In this light, the work in itself takes on a dynamic beauty and an inexhaustible power. If on the other hand religion

[10] A. 4, ad 1.
[11] Ad 2.
[12] P. 122.

in the eucharistic sacrifice and in the sacraments is looked on only as a subordinate purpose[13] and is ultimately considered not at all necessary for the attainment of the higher purpose, such a defective liturgical position lacks redeeming power. It loses its center. The forceful unity is missing.

Obviously, there are reasons to issue warnings against a superficial form of liturgy. The liturgical renewal successfully guarded itself against this danger for decades.

There was a first period of liturgical renewal in which it had especially to struggle to regain an appreciation of the inner fullness of meaning and comprehensibility of the holy signs. But today, in a second period, the great vision of the Church Fathers, which saw the entire Christian life including the theological virtues in the light of the saving mystery which comes to us in the sacraments, is winning out in the theology and piety of almost every country.

The liturgical renewal is no enemy to asceticism and contemplation. Rather it leads the celebrating community "to the heavenly Jerusalem, to the festal gathering and assembly of the first-born who are enrolled in heaven, to Jesus, the mediator of a new covenant" (Heb. 12, 22–24). It unites our life to the saving mysteries of the death and resurrection of Christ and thus demands an interior conformity with Christ the crucified. A liturgy celebrated in a beautiful and vital fashion also helps modern man, whom films and television have made so sensitive to the combination of seeing and hearing, out of his distraction to a contemplation that is proportionate to his nature. That, of course, also places high demands on catechesis, on the mystagogical sermon, and on liturgical formation. Word and sign must fuse into a genuine unity in order to draw men together as they emerge from the distractions of the world.

[13] Maritain writes, "Thus liturgical worship is in itself an end of very great dignity; and yet there is a higher end" (p. 101), which is wordless and signless contemplation.

The Significance of the Sacraments

THE Church Fathers were tireless in proclaiming love of neighbor, the spirit of community, saving solidarity as a task proceeding from the sacraments. There is no doubt that this is not
intended as an additional motivation that one can take or leave.
The sacraments by their nature impart a commission to sanctify
the social sphere. We must not slight this in proclamation, but
we must also not obscure the essential characteristic of the Christian law of morality, that is, that God first gives to us before he
demands: that the sacraments are first of all a gift of love and
then, and therefore, a commission. Only when the faithful become conscious through the proclamation that the sacraments are
of themselves a social, community-forming reality, will they also
grasp in the manner of the New Testament (that is, from the
spirit of love) the task of communal life flowing from them.
Nevertheless, as is generally true in the Christian life, more than
mere understanding is involved here: the sacraments must also
be celebrated and experienced in their external form as social
saving events. Then they will be effective forces forming the life
in the community.

THE SOCIAL-SALVATION CHARACTER OF THE SACRAMENTS IN THE CONSCIOUSNESS OF FAITH

It was not only in a rational way that the primitive Christian
community knew that the sacraments were connected to the

161

community; they grasped this truth in a living manner. Obviously, it is ultimately the action of the Holy Spirit which gives the living experience of faith. Yet we may also seek external reasons why the saving action of God uses secondary causes. When Ignatius of Antioch appealed to the Christians so earnestly and passionately to assemble around the altar and the bishop and to be conscious of this unity throughout their life, we can certainly hear in this the student of St. John, the evangelist of the sacraments, speaking out. But we can also feel his battle against threatening dissension and not least the immediate experience that the little Christian gathering could only withstand the attack of the heathen antispirit and persecution if they had the sign of unity and harmony before their eyes in the sacramental realm. As long as the Christian community was still of manageable size and celebrated the divine worship everywhere in a language comprehensible to everyone, the eucharistic symbol of the meal and the sacrificial meal was also a sign of community which spoke immediately, was experienced immediately. Christianity, constantly attacked from without and at the same time completely and entirely a mission Church, experienced with immediate force the fact that baptism gave her new members. So it followed from the external situation, but also from the spoken form of the baptismal celebration, that the celebrating community felt itself responsible for each baptized person, and that the baptized himself experienced himself as a vital, active member of the community, obligated to joint responsibility. The apostolic teaching of the saving unity of all the baptized in the mystical body of Christ (1 Cor. 12), of the kingdom of the priestly people of God, of the temple which raises itself out of living stones (1 Pet. 2, 5), remained vital in and through this very sacramental celebration.

The theology of the great scholastics has, in loyalty to tradition, presented the power of the sacraments for communal and unifying action with great clarity. But in their texts there is no longer that sound of immediate emotion that there was in Ignatius of Antioch, John of Jerusalem, Cyril of Alexandria, Chrysostom, Augustine, and other great theologians of the time of the Fathers.

The Gothic cathedral removes the altar too far from the people, and with its side naves and pillars primarily creates quiet corners for individual prayer. It might perhaps be argued that the Church could to some extent afford this deëmphasis on the community of those assembled about the altar just because at this time she most visibly achieved the power of informing the community. But could the liturgy thus also really in the long run retain the strength to hold together the communities of Christians and confirm it anew so that Christians might remain the leaven of all earthly social orders? This, then, was the attitude towards life of the *devotio moderna,* which has a greater feeling for the silent confrontation of the individual soul with Christ than for the community of his mystical body. Added to this was the aftereffect of nominalism, which curtailed the communal in favor of the individual. In brief, it was the feeling of the times of the late Middle Ages and early modern times which permitted the social-salvation side of sacramental theology and of the consciousness of faith in general to retreat more and more into the background. Finally, in the age of individualism it was more and more forgotten that the sacraments are a reality of social-salvation and that this fact must express itself as much in theology as in proclamation and in the formation of the sacramental celebration.

THEOLOGY, CONSCIOUSNESS OF FAITH, AND THE FORM OF SACRAMENTAL CELEBRATION

It is not out of a Neoplatonic schema of thought but rather an immediately experienced actuality in the divine worship that Augustine repeatedly preaches to us of the eucharist: " 'I am the

163

living bread which came down from heaven.' The faithful, if they do not reject it, know that they themselves are the body of Christ. Let them become the body of Christ, if they wish to live by the spirit of Christ. Only the body of Christ lives by the spirit of Christ. Do you wish to live by the spirit of Christ? Be in the body of Christ. For this reason the apostle explains this bread to us with the words: 'We many, being one bread, are one body' (1 Cor. 10, 17). O sacrament of love! O sign of unity! O bond of charity! He who wishes to live has that from which to live. Let him draw near, let him believe; let him be incorporated that he may be made to live. Let him not shrink from the fellowship of the members. Let him not be a deformed member of which one must be ashamed. Let him be a fit and sound member. Let him persevere in the body."[1]

Augustine could preach in such a manner because the people still responded unanimously in their *Amen* to the prayers of the priest, because they still heard the word of God spoken comprehensibly in the Mass, answered it, joined in the song of the priest, and ate the eucharistic meal together with the priest.

The symbol for the most extreme contradiction to the community which expresses itself in theology, preaching, and sacramental celebration is the communion of the faithful outside the Mass, which has almost become a rule in the past three centuries. The social dissolution of secular society is reflected here in frightening fashion. As the higher classes disdainfully detached themselves from the people—even the clergy often looked upon itself during and beyond the French Revolution primarily as a "privileged class"—the celebrating priest separated himself from the faithful, the "onlookers," by the spatial distance of the altar and still more by the Latin wall. As the messenger servants had to satisfy themselves in eating at their own servants' table—they were not counted among the family of their lord—so the faithful were satisfied "to be fed" normally outside the holy Mass. The

[1] Augustine, "Ad Jo. 26, 13," *PL* 35, 1612ff.

pious consoled themselves with thoughts which excluded almost all but the personal presence of Christ, the individual meeting with him, which is only a part of the whole truth. This kind of eucharistic celebration was accepted by the people without protest because it corresponded to the individualistic (and feudalistic) *Zeitgeist* and because even theology, and as a result the proclamation, unduly slighted the social-salvation side of the sacraments.

The celebration of baptism presented perhaps the saddest picture. Can we even speak of "celebration" at all? The baptisms in the hospital (and thus often outside the parish), the baptism at any hour of the day and in a hidden corner amid the presence of scarcely more than two or three persons stand in stark contrast to the early Christian baptismal celebration in the paschal vigil. Whereas in the consciousness of faith of the early Church and correspondingly also in the form of the baptismal celebration the "kingdom of priests, those dedicated to God, the consecrated people" were present and the entire Christian community celebrated the reception of the baptized into the people of God, the preaching and kind of baptismal formation in the nineteenth and even yet in the twentieth century often express only the partial truth of the hidden conferring of sanctifying grace on the individual soul. The form of the celebration lacks vitality and expresses the holy symbolic meaning of the sacraments, especially their social-salvation reality, only so imperfectly that the customary scholastic theology and preaching of the rich fullness of the sacramental world of faith is almost reduced to the mere question of the validity of matter and form, the severity of the commanded obligation, and the efficacy on the individual. Perhaps we have overstated the case. But no one will deny that such is the tendency.

Obviously, the sacraments in their immutable essence and in the ultimate care of their symbolic form remain ordered to the community, even if that is no longer felt. The erection of the community of salvation is at all times an essential fruit of the sacraments. Regardless of how the sacraments are celebrated, the saving solidarity of the entire Church is still within them. But the question is whether one is also conscious of this. There are, of course, always individual voices. Thus the moral theologian of Freising, Magnus Jocham, in the middle of the last century presented Catholic moral theology completely and entirely from the viewpoint of the mystical body of Christ and the sacraments.[2] But he found no echo.

Today we are experiencing powerful change; a new community consciousness is arising in the Church. One discovers with a new immediacy the manifold dimensions of Catholicity, which far exceed Western, not to say Latin cultural forms. The encyclical *Mystici corporis Christi* of Pius XII, which can be seen as a certain turning point in the conversion from salvation individualism to the mentality of social salvation, has found a strong echo in theology and piety. His encyclical *Mediator Dei* turned its attention to that character of the liturgy which is related to community without, of course, drawing the practical consequences boldly enough. In the early Christian manner it again refers to the eucharist as the "sign of unity, the bond of love, and the expression of harmony," and permits no doubt that the form of the divine worship should also express this character of community emphasis as clearly and impressively as possible.[3] Both scholarly theology and the proclamation as well as the liturgical renewal are making an effort to exhibit once again the communal character of the sacraments. The Second Vatican Council opened the door wide to a new era of the spirit of community in the understanding of the liturgy as much as in the entire structure of the Church.

[2] Magnus Jocham, *Moraltheologie oder die Lehre vom christlichen Leben*, 1852.
[3] *AAS*, 39, 1947, p. 566.

The Effect of the Sacraments on Social Life

The sacraments are Christ's bridal presents to his Church. It is through the sacraments and in them that the Church community lives.[4] The sacraments as *grace and commission* are gifts of the community, they are the foundation of the community and they bind one to her. "It is the communion of saints which dispenses the sacraments in the power of Christ. Every member of the Church is given a share in baptism, in the eucharist, in the remission of sins. The entire community stands around the dying faithful who attains perfect unity with Christ through the last anointing. The entire community surrounds those who work out their unity with Christ in the sacrament of marriage."[5] All graces which are the gifts of the sacraments indicate that there is an inner union with the community and a pressing obligation to cooperate in solidarity with the community of salvation.

The sacraments bring all that forth in a mysterious way, in which God himself is the ultimate efficient cause. The sacraments nevertheless do not act in the manner of magic, as perhaps through a senseless incomprehensible rite; God acts in them personally by means of the comprehensible sign and word,[6] the kerygmatic claims of grace, and the comprehensible commission. *The sacraments signify what they effect and effect what they signify.* Just as the word of the Father took flesh in the incarnation, Christ and the Church take on the sensible sign and the comprehensible word in the sacrament in order to bring forth the saving effects. It is a personal proceeding: a summons and interior capacity for response. Although the sacramental effect is not only of a psychological nature, it is nevertheless an essential part of the operating of the sacraments, which is at once visible

[4] See Thomas Aquinas, *Summa theol.* III, q. 65, a. 2, ad 3.

[5] M. Schmaus, *Katholische Dogmatik*, volume IV, part II, Munich, 1957, p. 83.

[6] See Romano Guardini, *Sacred Signs*.

167

and personal, that the psychological level (the immediate experience) not be neglected. We need not be surprised, therefore, if the community-forming strength of the sacraments is decreased the more the form of the celebration is individualistically diluted or falsified. Even if, in individual cases, the psychological mutilation of the sacramental power of expression does not call the validity of the administration into question, it can nevertheless set up an impediment to the full effectiveness of the sacraments.

The individualistic distortion of the sacramental celebration (the predominance of private baptisms, nondialogue Masses, etc.) parallels the slight degree of social integration and radiation of the congregation. If the truth of the social-salvation form of the sacraments is thoroughly neglected in the liturgy, the cohesion of the "parish community" will also be lacking in other areas; the spiritual preparation for a genuine community apostolate will be lacking; the societies and parish organizations will be extremely vulnerable to unfruitful rivalries and a dangerous particularism.

Common Task of Pastoral Liturgy and the Proclamation

We have attempted to show that the relations between theology, proclamation, liturgical celebration, and the *Zeitgeist* are reciprocal. It is the task of pastoral liturgy and proclamation, led by sound dogma, to assimilate what is sound in the *Zeitgeist* and to oppose the unsound by the power of faith. The drive towards the communal is coming to the fore in an extraordinary measure today, but it is mainly in the form of mere organization and an overpowering unspiritual collective. The liturgical renewal can turn the newly awakened understanding of community and society to advantage. But in this it must be aware of the danger of merely external organization: *it is not sufficient to organize a community worship externally.* Otherwise the external form could gradually assimilate itself to the likewise dangerous collec-

168

tive spirit of the surrounding society. The sacraments act as intelligible words and signs. Therefore, the external form of divine worship must also go hand in hand with the catechesis and preaching on the social-salvation form and the social-salvation commission of the sacraments and of the Christian life in general.

The mere explanation of the social-salvation imperative of the sacraments, on the other hand, will have only a very qualified success if the social-salvation gift of grace of the sacraments is not at the same time clearly expressed through the liturgical celebration.

The attempt to make the Latin language the exclusive and universal language of the liturgy—even extending to the unfortunate attempt at the Latinization of the Uniates and the establishing of Latin patriarchates in the areas with Eastern rites —was, of course, not simply a product of Western cultural colonialism; it was in a way also an attempt to give expression to the all-encompassing community of the Church in the sacraments. But outside the area of the Romance languages this attempt achieves neither the wonderful experience of the first feast of Pentecost, when all understood the same message in their own tongues, nor the full community-forming power in relation to the local parishes; for an incomprehensible language does not bind together those celebrating in the same way that the mother tongue does. The unity and community of the Catholic Church must also be built up from below in a subsidiary fashion.

If today the Church so energetically encourages the utmost use of the vernacular in dispensing the sacraments, then we may doubtless suppose that this, like the new sacramental life breaking forth throughout the Church, is a *gift of the pentecostal spirit which joins the bond of unity in all sacraments and through them.* The Holy Spirit acts through words and signs understandable to us. It is our task in loyalty to his work and to the holy Church, the bride of the Holy Spirit, to give the liturgical signs

169

and words their full undiminished social-salvation power of expression. Then we may not doubt that the Spirit of love by these means will also gather together those who are separated and bestow on the community of the Church the attractive power of love.

TIME OF UNBELIEF

Lack of Faith and the Environment

FAITH is an entirely personal decision, a personal encounter of man with God revealing himself and with his truth; it is a response of man which claims heart and will, understanding and spirit. No one can take this personal decision away from man; no one can force him to believe. But if, as is absolutely indispensable, we stress the personal character of the decision of faith, we must not overlook the fact that faith of its innermost essence is at the same time also a social phenomenon.

From the beginning faith comes to the individual as a reality which is also social: it is mediated to him in its content and in its clearness by the Church. He receives faith, like baptism, from the Church (baptismal rite). It is always the concrete community of the family, of the neighborhood, of the parish, etc., which brings the first experience of faith to the individual. The vitality of the faith in the environment partly determines the vitality of the faith of the individuals. This fact not only has its basis in the psychological and social formation of man, but also corresponds to the mysterious saving solidarity of the members of the mystical body of Christ. The more a believer consciously and joyfully mediates the witness of faith to his environment, so much the more his own faith deepens, and the more intimately he takes part in the community of faith. This community unites

173

men more effectively and more permanently than any mere community of interests.

Can it then be said: Like faith, its opposite, unbelief, is also simultaneously an entirely personal decision and a social phenomenon? Yes, but only in the sense of an analogy, not in the sense of an equality; for unbelief does not in any way have the pronounced personal physiognomy of faith; nor does unbelief create a personal community in the real sense, but only a collective of men which suffers more and more from the loss of personal self-determination and personal assimilation of values. Faith permits men to come to themselves and at the same time to find the Thou of the other and the We of the community. Unbelief, on the other hand, locks man within himself, impoverishes him, doles out to him mass feelings and collective opinions.

It is not only those outside the Church but also the faithful through their public denial who cooperate in this worldly corrupt force of unbelief. If disbelief is to be overcome, it is here that the battle can and must first be begun.

THE SCANDAL OF THE "BELIEVING" ENVIRONMENT

There are two ways in which a more or less believing environment can be guilty of the disbelief of individuals and of the dechristianization of an entire milieu; these correspond to the two basic forms in which the unbelief appears. Negative unbelief (in which case a man does not believe because he has not yet actually been confronted with the decision on faith) stems largely from the fact that the so-called believing environment gave no shining convincing witness of faith. Positive unbelief (the culpable and conscious decision against faith) always has its direct foundation in the free will of this unbelieving man who has closed himself to the grace and truth of God; nevertheless, because of the mysterious salvation solidarity of men, the guilt

174

of others, especially the scandal of the faithful, can also play a disastrous role.

The Unconvincing Celebration of the "Mysterium Fidei"

The celebration of the eucharist (and with it the entire sacramental celebration) is the *mysterium fidei,* the mystery continuing the faith of the Church and awakening the faith of men. But if formalism and spiritlessness have made the celebration of faith unconvincing and incomprehensible, if the priest at the altar is hasty and thoughtless and the community of faithful in practice does not participate at all in the mystery of the Church confessing the faith, then the unbeliever, along with those Christians who are baptized but who still have not attained a consciousness of the baptismal reality, will not be led by such a "celebration" to faith or to a more vital faith.

St. Paul warns the Corinthians that they should speak in comprehensible language at the gathering for worship: "If, therefore, the whole Church assembles and all speak in tongues, and outsiders or unbelievers enter, will they not say that you are mad?" (1 Cor. 14, 23).

If the worship in all our churches were really also experientially and perceptibly the *mysterium fidei,* the meaningful and joyous expression of our faith and the community of faith, perhaps many of those souls, so close to unbelief, who only attend Sunday services from force of habit, would be led by the witness of a happy believing community to a more vital faith and would in the end preserve their faith. It must be said that the dechristianization of the milieu did not come first of all from the middle class, from films and press, from the trade-unions and political parties, but rather before that from the kind of liturgical celebration which was in contradiction to the *mysterium fidei.*

175

This is even more true when there is added to a formalistic, even scandalous, service a proclamation of the word which is so frozen in scholastic formulas that it is no longer able to speak to modern man. All this not only means a deplorable falling off of the witness of faith, but it can become for many active men a real scandal which seduces them into taking a position against the Church and faith.

If everyone wrote the history of his faith, or lack of faith, we might perhaps read many sentences like the following from the autobiography of the Swedish convert Sven Stolpe:[1] "The real cause of this entirely unproblematic rejection of Christianity was, I felt, our religion teacher in school. From all my schoolmates I heard confirmation of his extraordinary talent of turning his students away from Christianity." On his path to conversion the encounter with a true Christian played a decisive role, yet the lack of witness of faith in the liturgy made his way to the Church not an easy one: "I saw priests read Mass with such lack of spirituality, such indifference and indolence, that it required my entire tenacity not to despair."

The *mysterium fidei* which Christians celebrate in the eucharist and in all sacraments is intended to make them witnesses to the faith for their environment. ". . . that you may declare the wonderful deeds of him who called you out of darkness into his marvelous light" (1 Pet. 2, 9). Out of the *centrum fidei*, the eucharist, the whole life should be formed and become a witness of faith to the environment. The unbelieving, who cannot experience the mystery of baptism and the eucharist, should be led by the life of Christians, which is nourished by these mysteries, to the mystery itself. But if the life of the priest and of Christians stands in contradiction to the celebration of faith, it would mean a loss to the environment of the witness of faith, of the belief-inspiring power, and not seldom a positive scandal which shares in the blame for the disbelief of others. Let us listen again to

[1] Sven Stolpe, *Warum wir katholisch wurden,* Heidelberg.

176

Sven Stolpe: "The few examples of Christian faith which I observed seemed so Pharisaical to me that they could only influence me negatively."

Behind the façade of a superficially traditional Christianity there hides a widespread and unseparated half-faith and unbelief. An external storm can then reveal what was genuine and what not. But a vitalization which awakens and enkindles the faith of one can also bring to the light of day the already latent disbelief of another. What is of itself God's external instrument of grace is for many the occasion for a deeper fall. A pastor who was singularly successful in vitalizing a parish through the eucharist after almost twenty years of untiring pastoral work, once said to us when we expressed our great joy over the public spirit of faith in the parish: "But do not overlook the other side, please; so many who were earlier ready to participate in a well-tempered Christianity have now separated themselves from the life of the Church."

The Practically Unbelieving Talk in the Environment

The progressing estrangement from the faith and the incipient disbelief of many people results not least from what is for practical purposes unbelieving talk in the environment. Often the disbelieving or the half-believing contribute in the same way. The investigations of pastoral sociology in the past years have made it frighteningly clear how widely even those who still go to church speak for all practical purposes with disbelief at work, in the neighborhood, at home. Men speak no longer of providence but of fate; they desire a sudden death in which they are aware of nothing; at New Year's they no longer wish God's blessing for one another but talk of health and fortune; upon the remarriage of a divorced person it is remarked, "How can you expect a man to live alone in his best years?"; a divorce

177

and remarriage, like premarital intercourse, are defended; the sacrifice of the fathers and mothers of large families is ridiculed; those who are successful in business are glorified, even when it is known that their practices conform neither to love nor to justice. What is bad is that the good do not often have the courage to contradict or even to attempt to speak believingly of the basic things.

It may be possible to say the creed in the Church (or to attend a kind of worship which does not demand a terribly radical witness of faith) for a long time and yet outside to accept unchristian speech silently and without protest, and begin little by little to converse and even to think without faith. But in the long run either the creed of the divine service or the unbelieving talk and thought and conduct outside must prevail. The Christian must realize that the sincere celebration of the eucharist and the other sacraments obligates him in his very heart to illumine his environment by faith. This is not only a commandment but also a presupposition for the vitality of his own faith.

The practically unbelieving talk one hears constantly in one's environment strengthens its sinister seducing power still more by what one reads in various circumstances in the newspapers, in illustrated weeklies and magazines, and by what one hears and sees on television and radio. Even if all this does not directly work against faith, in the final analysis it places before our eyes a world in which faith no longer plays any role at all, which makes it indeed a powerful antithesis to those short hours of Sunday spent in the full light of faith (if not in a formalistic, repugnant service).

Of course, it is no decree of blind fate that the milieu must disintegrate the faith of the individual; there is no inevitable "mechanism of dechristianization." Man is by his nature designed and obligated to confront his milieu actively; of its innermost essence faith demands confession in the milieu, a confession in which the individual should not isolate himself but rather should unite with the faithful in his area. Even in the environment which seems to form the most unfavorable climate imaginable for a joyous spirit of faith, the active, apostolically oriented Christian—and only he—can behave quite differently in a sincere alliance with others of like mind. The slight power of Christians in their environment bears more than a slight portion of the guilt for the shallow faith or lack of faith of many. Because today they do not effectively profess to their environment the faith still present in them, they themselves degenerate tomorrow into half-belief and finally into unbelief.

The Seductive Power of Conscious Disbelief

It would be an error to trace back every disbelief to a mere misunderstanding or to a scandal given by the faithful. Certainly, the *diabolos,* the confuser, also is partial to using the sins and superficialities of the faithful, but it is the unbelievers who actually form his army.

One section of men is attracted to unbelief by the "freedom" which it promises. These men allege themselves to be those who are able to enjoy the good life and all beautiful things unimpeded. The naïve do not notice how the new false gods (economic prosperity, higher standard of living, unimpeded pleasure of the senses) behave more and more like inhuman masters.

The "Father of Lies" attracts others to whom propriety, self-control, and social performance are significant by means of those men so adept at unbelief who seek to appease their own bad consciences by living more blamelessly, controlling themselves better, undertaking more social works than their believing neighbors. Perhaps there are "negative unbelievers" of genuine idealism; as such and as individuals they are something positive; but taken together they nevertheless stand behind a minus sign because they are "yoked with the false." "He who does not gather with me scatters" (Lk. 11, 23). Even the Gnostic mythos knew

179

that the daemons seize greedily on bits of light, for their anti-kingdom cannot be built out of dark elements alone.

Disbelief seeks to impress itself forcibly on the fanatic and the emphatically strong-willed by the inflexibility and directness of a life without God, by the titanic defiance and the radical denial of every religious impulse. On the other hand, to a gentler disposition it preaches tolerance as the uppermost principle: nothing is more stigmatized than a stubborn insistence on a truth. Unbelievers assert patronizingly that they gladly permit religion to Christians as a private affair if only they would not intolerantly try to place everyone under the claims of their religion. As an unbeliever one can dispute on every subject and eclecticize from everything; but Christianity is the quintessence of intolerance.

The intensity of the temptation occasioned by unbelief depends largely on the guise in which it confronts the individual in his sphere of life. Nevertheless, it is decisive that faith in the same environment utterly destroys the deception of unbelief by the force of its radiance. "This is the victory that overcomes the world, our faith" (1 Jn. 5, 4). Unbelief not infrequently presents itself in the garments of real values, especially those which speak to the *Zeitgeist*. The less Christians exert themselves to redeem the true and the good in the *Zeitgeist* and to bring them to validity in purified form, the greater will be the illusion of these partial values seized upon and distorted by disbelief. The believing man must not merely give witness to a timeless truth, he must rather so live the saving truths in his time and in his environment and so witness to them that their delivering and liberating power comes fully to the consciousness of those tempted by unbelief.

180

The Encounter with the *Zeitgeist*

THE CHRISTIAN SPIRIT OF COMMUNITY IN THE ENCOUNTER
WITH THE "ZEITGEIST"

By *Zeitgeist,* or spirit of the time, we mean the general perceptible summation of the opinions, purposes, and states of mind
of a particular age. The *Zeitgeist* is distinguished from what we
might call the *Zeit-Ungeist,* or antispirit of the time, in that it
always bears within itself the intense vitality of youth. It is
usually concerned with announcing some new thing, some new
idea, that has caught the imagination and seems to express the
sentiments of the generation. We must take care, therefore, not
to equate the *Zeitgeist* carelessly with the *Zeit-Ungeist,* which
is an oppressive force that goes directly against the spirit of the
age.

Though the *Zeitgeist* of a period is more definable once it has
passed and can therefore be seen in historical perspective—for
example, the "spirit of reason" in the seventeenth century, of the
"nation" and "revolution" in the eighteenth, of "science" in the
nineteenth—it has nevertheless many tangible properties, and
can have a powerful and even recognizable influence on a
civilization.

The typical defenders of the traditional, the stubborn representatives of the older generation of any period, that is to say, the bearers of the *Zeit-Ungeist*, are inclined to damn the *Zeitgeist* root and branch beforehand. Christian principles, however, forbid this. *For every age belongs to God.* Every age with its own proper *Zeitgeist* conceals within itself life-bearing elements. Every age calls for the truth which will redeem it, for the values which will fulfill its yearnings. If one does not listen to the summons of the *Zeitgeist* or rejects it roughly, he should not be surprised if he is controlled by the antispirit and errors of the time. Such a way of acting means not only a hopeless need for the original *Zeitgeist,* but also a disastrous loss in strength for the advocate of truth. If on one side, then, stand the errors of the time, which have assimilated the power of the age's attitude towards life, on the other side there stands perhaps a group of people weary of life who cover themselves externally with the shield of "eternal truths," but who in their innermost being are characterized by a hoary *Zeitgeist* of a declining epoch, and, finally, unsuspecting, are handed over to the virus by the *misled Zeitgeist* of yesterday and today. The ever young and never failing power of immutable truths reveals itself only in the positive fruitful encounter with the *Zeitgeist,* and not in mere retreat to the past.

The Christian who is not content with uncomprehended formulas and customs but is deeply at home in truth can risk taking his stand with the *Zeitgeist.* He is able to listen to all the good in it; and because he stresses the "old and new" from the treasure of inherited truth—the old in a new manner—he gains an intimate relationship to the immutable truth and makes the warm breath of the *Zeitgeist* his own stimulus.

Salvation history operates in the area of temporal history. The present and the future belong only to those who are dedicated at the same time to the full truth and to the progress of history. For those, on the other hand, who seek to hold fast to the forms of yesterday as the epitome of the enduring, there remains eventually only the dross of the *Zeitgeist,* vital at one time, but now burned out, and dead formulas which once had a deep life-giving meaning, but have now become routine or mean something completely different and thus prevent a healthy perspective of truth.

It is the task of the faithful to effect a distinction within the *Zeitgeist* itself through "the sword of faith," through the radiating good news. This is part of the eschatological mission of Christendom. Only when the good news finds the alert ear of the time and knows how to speak to its deepest longings can the light of the gospel illumine all values and completely unmask the darkness. The innermost thoughts should rather be manifested by the power of the truth vitally proclaimed and the faith vitally lived.

The distinction or separation presupposes that good, less good, and evil are mixed together, are interwoven. A positive encounter of Christendom with the *Zeitgeist* is founded on the belief that God's mercy and wisdom is at work everywhere in some manner until the last great day of separation at the return of the Lord. It is good to uncover the seeds of truth and see that often it is these seeds, much more than the naked error, which give a current of an age its impetus and attraction for men. Christians, therefore, may not act towards the *Zeitgeist* like that servant who at the weeding out of the cockle also wished to trample the entire wheat crop.

CATHOLIC MORAL THEOLOGY IN THE ENCOUNTER WITH THE "ZEITGEIST"

There was a time when the passion with which the Christian laity of antiquity followed the great discussions on the basic truths of faith aroused only a sympathetic smile. The more or less liberal middle-class citizen was of the opinion that questions of theology and the proclamation of doctrines of faith and morals were of interest to theologians exclusively. It is a good sign for our time that the Catholic laity are again taking a vital part in the stirring questions of theology. They do not want a superficial "theology of the laity," which according to the words of Pius XII[1] is itself a contradiction in terms, alongside the theology of priests; they wish as formed Christians of the twentieth century to penetrate as deeply as possible into the mystery of the faith and the foundations of moral doctrine. With especially lively interest the formed laity as well as the pastoral clergy are following today's endeavors to deepen moral theology and to adapt it to the special needs of our time. Such laity, believing deeply and glowing with apostolic zeal, who by their high demands upon the proclamation of moral doctrine force the pastors and theologians to deeper reflection and to a genuine encounter with the world of today, are not uncommon.

Theology, too, and not least of all moral theology, regularly undergoes its "clash of generations." The more clearly that it is itself conscious of the problem, the less danger will there be. Someone understanding theology as a merely static transmission of unalterable truth will—apart from many other misunderstandings—be tempted to play off the theologians of yesterday and today against one another. He will interpret the service of today's theology of salvation history as an assault upon the theology of yesterday. What was conditioned theologically and culturally by the modes of expressions and presentation of yesterday's theological problems will perhaps be obstinately defended by him as an enduring inheritance.

It is quite natural that moral theology in a time of profound social and cultural change carries on the discussion with the *Zeitgeist* more consciously and takes the altered social conditions as an occasion to think through many problems anew. In no other way can it fulfill its service to salvation faithfully. But at the same time it must not endanger the continuity of theological work and with it the purity of tradition. An intensified dialogue

[1] An address of May 31, 1954; see *AAS*, 46, 1954, pp. 313–317.

with the *Zeitgeist* demands a deepened knowledge of the sources and an unquestioning loyalty towards tradition. That again requires a systematic attention to the patterns of earlier theological work, which follow from the function of theology in salvation history. Only when we know the intellectual and social physiognomy of the time in which the earlier theologians fulfilled their service will we be just to them, will we understand their concerns and their language and learn from them to fulfill our task of today in consummate loyalty to tradition.

A theology which thinks and speaks exclusively in the language and frame of reference of a past epoch without taking into consideration the transformations of time, unconsciously falsifies many statements of earlier theologians; it finds no echo in its time, it is no beacon for those spiritual currents of the time which are searching for the saving truth; it might better be compared to the "light under the bushel." While it seeks to save itself from the sharp windy draft of present intellectual currents in the world of traditional formulas, it is also losing contact with yesterday's intellectual parents; the time-conditioned which it absolutizes hangs on its garment like a musty odor.

The conflict between the generations in theology is resolved and is always fruitful anew if in its eternal youth it is open in equal measure to tradition and to the questions of the time. Theology must be of every time: a proclamation of the eternal truth in the language of the time, a service to salvation in complete openness to the needs and the positive strengths of the time.

THE "SAVING SOLIDARITY" OF MARXISM AND THE INDIVIDUALISM OF CHRISTIANS

It is not unjust to call Marxism the last cry of a God-alienated humanism which knows almost nothing of the true value of man. An intellectual system which derives all its opinions of human life only from below, from the economic organization of society

185

as a whole, subordinates man to the conditions of production. This shameful collectivism is a trampling of individuality, of the family and every mature community into a heartless organization of slavery. But the other side must also not be overlooked: In proletarian Marxism, not only does a pseudo-religious expectation of the earthly paradise lead the eternal yearning for the fulfillment of all things into error; there are also awakened in it amazing powers of solidarity and sacrificial courage. Unnumbered workers have accepted in faith the teachings of Karl Marx, according to which they must take upon themselves the hard law of a constantly increasing pauperization of the proletariat, without striving for any alleviation or mitigation of social antitheses, in order to open the way to the classless paradise for future generations. Men who might well have become saints if they had been challenged radically enough for the kingdom of God felt themselves repelled by the shabby egotistical worry about salvation of some Christians who only looked after the saving of their own souls without effectively throwing themselves into the work for the kingdom of God.

In the face of this erring saving solidarity in Marxism, Catholic moral theology of today cannot avoid an examination of conscience: Have we always understood the teaching of conversion as shown by the Lord, as a turning to the kingdom of God, to his dominion of love which establishes community? Christ clearly connected the joyous knowledge of the return home to God, of conversion, to the demand of the kingdom of God upon us: "The time is fulfilled, and the kingdom of God is at hand; repent, and believe in the gospel" (Mk. 1, 15). It is a deep shame for Christendom of the nineteenth and early twentieth centuries that the early Christian expectation of the redemption of all mankind and all things was shown more ardently and with greater solidarity in the degenerated expectation of salvation of Marxism than in the life of salvation-egotistical Christians. This also presents a question for those treatises of moral theology which had precious little to say of the coming of the kingdom of God in this world and of the praiseworthy commission of saving solidarity given to every baptized and confirmed person for the kingdom of God.

It may perhaps be asserted that present-day moral theology, especially since the encyclical *Mystici corporis Christi*,[2] struggles resolutely to bring out more clearly the saving-solidarity aspect of Christian morality in individual demands as well as in its over-all presentation. The "priestly" people of God, the baptized and confirmed, once again understand with very different ardor that the salvation of the individual lies in his contribution to the kingdom of God, and that Christian hope thinks not only of the salvation of one's own soul—although certainly of that, too—but burns just as much for the salvation of all men. More attention is again paid to the deep sense of those words of Paul which offer a comprehensive motivation of Christian morality: "There is one body and one Spirit, just as you were called to the one hope" (Eph. 4, 4). The stronger eschatological orientation of moral theology attempts again, as it did in Christian antiquity, to make perceptible the fact that we await in common the coming of the Lord, the new heaven and the new earth. The entire Christian life is characterized by this.

If Marxism awaits the final salvation of mankind by the progress of technology and the improvement of production conditions and thus sees salvation come nearer with every new Sputnik and with every social reform in Communist Russia, so Catholic moral theology must, on the other hand, not only warn of the truth that salvation comes from God alone and man remains man truly only if he lives from the love of God, but today it must also apply a theology of earthly realities more emphatically than in the nineteenth century. The social task of the individual and the community and the entire social order of human society are considered anew in the light of revelation.

[2] *AAS*, 35, 1943, pp. 193–248.

SECULAR ETHICS AND THE LAW OF CHRIST

A comparison of the *manualia theologiae moralis*, more or less typical since the seventeenth century, with the newer treatises on moral theology establishes satisfactorily that the younger generation no longer has a taste for presentations of Christian morality which sometimes seem more like collections of laws than like the gospel. Today men again wish to see the Christian life radically from its one and only center, from life in Christ. Does that perhaps mean that we of today are more devout, more pious than earlier moral theologians? By no means! In those days, if we do not deceive ourselves, they could still afford to instruct the future father confessors by simply setting forth and offering reasons for the individual norms and duties. The primacy of grace, life from the mysteries of salvation, the Christian imprint upon the entire existence—all this was, so to speak, still something obvious, or it still seemed to be.

For this same reason, the present day demands a much deeper and more basic consideration of the roots of Christian morality in the gracious joining of man with Christ, in the saving mystery of the Church, and in the holy sacraments, because to the man of today in the midst of a profane world and a secular interpretation of life it is no longer so obvious that the roots of the moral life are to be sought in faith and in grace. The degenerate *Zeitgeist* of secularism is an inexorable challenge to moral theology to distinguish itself more sharply from a mere teaching of duty in the manner of the Stoics or Kant and to produce the full wealth of the Christian life as a life with God—and this must be done not only in ascetical literature, but in scholarly moral theology itself.

As long as the secular ethic admits the validity of a morality based upon the natural law, we will not fall into the error of reacting to it by an insufficient, incomplete supranaturalism. We will prevail over secular naturalism in ethics and the profane interpretation of the world only as we work out more clearly the unity of the law of grace and the natural moral law in the "law of Christ" (Gal. 6, 2).

TWO DIFFERENT FORMS OF PERSONALISM

The *Zeitgeist* is not something absolutely uniform. On the contrary, it shows very different currents; extreme assertions in one direction are often matched by their opposite extremes, either simultaneously or as subsequent reactions. Against the constantly growing danger of collectivism a spontaneous emphasis on the worth of the personality is stirring, a strong intellectual current which is generalized into the term "personalism." In the past years, this concept was used to designate very different intellectual movements which have little in common outside their common aversion to the massing by collectives and the despiritualizing by bureaucracy. Repeated assertions of Pope Pius XII against an anthropomorphic personalism tending towards self-glorification were employed by a few moralists, who obviously had no contact with the great Catholic currents of the time, as weapons against a direction in moral theology which calls itself *personalism* with much more justice than that egocentric humanism condemned by the supreme teacher of Christendom. Thus it is worthwhile to distinguish the two clearly.

A false personalism, for example, sees marriage as especially or even exclusively a possibility for developing all "personal" values. In this the stress lies strongly on the values of sensual pleasure and one's own satisfaction. Egotism, which conceals itself under the high name of "personalism," can be seen, for example, in the widespread interpretation which suggests that when it is clear to a person that the preservation of his marriage

189

no longer contributes to the development of his "personality," then he has the right and perhaps even the duty to dissolve it and seek for himself a partner from whom he can expect a greater advancement for his "personality."[3]

Here we are obviously concerned with the degeneration of a current of the times. Should Catholic moral theology, in violent reaction to such a degeneration, withdraw to a teaching of norms and duties which is purely object-related? The numerous representatives of Catholic personalism, in any case, think otherwise. It is truly worthwhile, in this time of technology, of all too purposeful thought and a one-sided objectivization, to hear fully the longing hidden in the living *Zeitgeist* for a warmer, more human, and more personal understanding of the moral life.

Catholic personalism—to whose present character there have, of course, also been contributions by a few non-Catholics such as Martin Buber[4] and Emil Brunner,[5] but which nevertheless is obliged for its strongest stimulus to such Catholic thinkers as Ferdinand Ebner,[6] Theodor Steinbüchel,[7] Romano Guardini,[8] and many others—is completely connected with the holy Scriptures. It is a biblical personalism of love. The value of the human person is seen as coming from God. The primitive Christian truth of man as an image of God is developed with passionate love. This personalism of love does not stand in opposition to community; on the contrary, it shows the person as related to the community in his roots. It is perhaps the most

[3] The book on marriage by Ernst Michel, condemned by the Holy Office, is a typical example of this tendency.

[4] M. Buber, *Dialogisches Leben*, 1943; *Das Problem des Menschen*, 1948; *Urdistanz und Beziehung*, 1951.

[5] E. Brunner, *Der Mensch im Widerspruch*, 1937; see H. Volk, *E. Brunners Lehre von der ursprünglichen Gottebenbildlichkeit des Menschen*, 1939.

[6] F. Ebner, *Wort und Liebe*, 1935; *Das Wort und die geistigen Realitäten*, 1952. See T. Steinbüchel, *Der Umbruch des Denkens*, 1936.

[7] T. Steinbüchel, *Mensch und Wirklichkeit in Philosophie und Dichtung des 20. Jh.*, 1949; *Der Zerfall des christlichen Ethos im 19. Jh.*, 1951.

[8] R. Guardini, *Christliches Bewusstsein*, 1935; *Freiheit, Gnade, Schicksal*, 1948; *Welt und Person*, 1950.

powerful expression of solidarity. The personality expands through loving service of neighbor and community by virtue of its inner law of being.

The biblical personalism of love in no way dissolves the norms, but it is anxiously concerned not to make of them a dead law between God and man. Personalism also wishes to present love by its whole manner of expression as a living personal demand, as a call to community. It sees the standard of behavior in the loving gifts of God. Above all, general and individual existence is understood as a gift of divine love which brings to us the commission of God. Because the commission comes to us through the living gift, the first demand of all is that love be given as a response which looks not only to the I itself, but to the Thou and the community. Morality is also expressed in spoken form as a dialogue between God and man; it is the response to the summons of Christ.

This biblical personalism is especially connected with Pauline thought. Not the individual laws contemplated for themselves, but the law of Christ, the love of God come to us personally in Christ, forms the basic theme with which every individual question is impressed. Christ is again experienced more clearly in the total presentation of moral theology as "the way, the truth, and the life." The first signs of a moral systematic in Clement of Alexandria, who designated the natural ethic of the heathens as "seeds of the Word" and thus displayed the unity of natural and supernatural revelation, the unity of natural moral law and Christ's demand for grace, find visible vindication in the development of Catholic scripturally grounded personalism.

ERRORS AND CONCERNS OF EXISTENTIALISM

The repugnant sides of an existentialism *à la* Sartre have been acutely exhibited during the past years: its lack of understanding for the enduring essential structure and the demands of struc-

191

tures, its flight into the unstructured and lawless, the confusion of freedom and caprice. Corresponding to the instructions of the supreme teacher of the Church and the Holy Office, the moral theologians of all lands are rightly emphasizing that the immutable moral norms are to be presented clearly as a contrast to the existential dissolution of law (in false situation ethics). This same tendency can be seen in the numerous positions that were taken by Pius XII on important and relevant moral problems.

That is, however, only the one side of the moral theological task in the face of existentialism's most disparate stamp. Even the most perverted existentialism means a summons for us to examine our consciences. If the lazy situation ethics is the breaking down of the commonly binding law (in the direction of the Pauline "*sarx*"), then it can certainly not be overcome by a morality which mistakenly stresses the establishment of the legal minimum or is a mere compilation of various moral and legal obligations. In the face of the false situation ethics it is especially worthwhile to work out the deep basis and unity of the moral norms in dogma, in being and life. If the existentialist falsely imagines the Christian morality as a mere multitude of imperatives foreign to life, then today's moral theology must present the law of Christ with passionate emphasis as a law of grace, as a "law of the Spirit of life in Christ Jesus" (Rom. 8, 2). It is not a law of set limits; it is a law of life that urges towards constant growth in the good.

The situation ethicist, who is stamped by the fundamental attitude of a distorted existentialism, loves the risk; but he knows nothing of the ultimate joyful significance which lies in the use of his freedom. The Catholic moral theologian of today must show lovingly how, in the Christian truth of the freedom of the children of God who follow in everything the guidance of the Holy Spirit and who hear in every gift of God a living summons to response, —how freedom of the will and man's

192

initiative are valued much more highly. To the cowardly flight into the unstructured, the evasion of the law by situation ethicists, we contrast the Christian ethos of loyalty to an inviolable fundamental law and the sensitivity to the summons of the hour and the courage to be heroic.

THE "ZEITGEIST" OF BUREAUCRACY AND JURIDICISM

The battle of existentialist situation ethics is directed expressly against every essential law only by its most extreme advocates. Simply a denial of formulated law is to be attributed to most. If in this they are not able to distinguish between purely positive law, which is adaptable and indeed often does need adaptation, and the permanently enduring law of being, then those moralists who press the Christian moral doctrine into a kind of codex and even sometimes portray the natural law as if it were no more than a list of statements formulated once for all, are also guilty. In *vitalism, personalism*, and *existentialism*, vehement reactions rise up against a threatening bureaucratization of life. It is especially worthwhile to understand what is true in this protest and to free it from possible errors. It is not through the mere rejection of the false and through warning of dangers, but through fulfillment of genuine concerns through the eternal treasures of Catholic truth that one meets the dangers of the *Zeitgeist* most successfully in the long run.

Moral theology has not infrequently been criticized in the past three centuries for its relative overgrowth in the treatment of purely legal problems. It is reproached for treating even the purely moral questions more or less according to the methods of jurisprudence. But for a just criticism two facts must be kept in mind. First, the moral theologians of the time were compelled to take upon themselves in their textbooks completely legal problems because there was unfortunately still no general ecclesiastical lawbook. The second thing to be said is that the presentation of

193

a noble-minded Christian life according to the law of grace was in no way slighted by the great moral theologians of past epochs. Thus Alphonsus of Liguori, besides his great moral theology, which dealt with the office of confessor, wrote many other, more broadly circulated ascetical works. For example, in his *The Love of Jesus Christ*[9] he presents the entire Christian life in conjunction with 1 Corinthians 13 from the viewpoint of love.

If the contemporary critique of moral theology of the past centuries is partly of the opinion that in the "juridicizing of morality" the *Zeitgeist* in some way reflects the absolutist form of government of society of that day, then this is in any case a warning for the present generation to take care in all efforts towards renewal not to succumb to the currents of the *Zeitgeist* by a dangerous assimilation. On the other hand, even the positive effort to trace the true concerns of the *Zeitgeist* and to exhibit their fulfillment in Christian truth clearly—and, of course, in a form which is most easily accessible to men today—will necessarily dispose men towards a more gentle criticism of earlier moral theology. For earlier theology also must be judged by its serving function for *its* time. Very many characteristics of moral theology of the past centuries, as for example the passionate discussions on the so-called moral systems which were established mainly as a result of the confused legal situation, and the theory of purely penal laws of the state, receive a positive meaning if one bears in mind the sociological condition of the time.

Finally, it must also be remembered that the manuals of moral theology written for confessors, which were never intended to be exhausted presentations of Catholic moral teaching, could in earlier centuries presume much more Christian substance than is permitted to us today. Anyone who knows history, for example, knows what urgent needs of the time were met by the *ratio studiorum* of the Society of Jesus, which stood at the

[9] New York, Herder and Herder, 1966, with a Preface by Bernard Häring.

194

cradle of the moral theology oriented primarily to the confessional. In the complications after the Reformation and Counterreformation the concern to train qualified confessors was urgent.

An extremely mistaken reaction to bureaucratism and the danger of juridicism would be the neglect of the legal structure of the Church and the retreat of moral theology to the merely general law of being. Of course, after the appearance of the *Codex Juris Canonici* and many excellent textbooks of canon law, the content of canon law need not be treated any longer by moral theology. The canonists with justice would dismiss this as an interference in their discipline and as a sign of mistrust. But moral theology today must try that much more to show the ultimate meaning of the positive ecclesiastical and secular laws and their arrangement in the law of Christ. The connections between justice and moral theology must be treated penetratingly in the face of bureaucracy as well as of a *Zeitgeist* dangerously inimical to law. Just as the separation of the Church of justice from the Church of love means laceration of the *one* foundation and bride of Christ, so too life in the law of grace and obedience to the positive laws of the Church may not stand unconnected alongside one another. The concern here is above all the infusing of meaning, of a spirit into the structure. The style used by moral theology to present the positive laws of the Church and the state and of obedience to authority must clearly detach itself from the bureaucratic style of a corrupt *Zeitgeist*. The legal element in the Church gets its significance from the theological, from the understanding of the Church as a community of love in the time of diaspora and attack.

THE ANSWER TO THE SLOGAN "RELIGION IS A PRIVATE AFFAIR"

What liberalism and socialism have often patronizingly tried to present to Christians as a remedy against "clericalism" and as a grand charter of toleration—the axiom "Religion is a private affair"—is in reality the worst blasphemy of our century. There is no doubt that this slogan expresses a powerful current of the present-day *Zeitgeist*, one to which many Christians, too, are not automatically immune. Even before the enemies of Christianity took up this slogan as a weapon, there were all too many Christians who did not grasp that their responsibility in the social sphere stood as much under the claim of God's dominion as did their private lives. There were confessional guides which named almost all imaginable sins of the private life but scarcely a sin against the social order. An entrepreneur of the last century might confess his little daily sins with extreme scrupulosity without even thinking of his enormous social responsibility.

Even the texbooks on moral theology did not always devote adequate attention to responsibility in social questions. Nevertheless, before one raises an unjustly generalized accusation one must also keep in mind here the changed social situation. When the type of moral theology which has predominated for close to three centuries came into fashion, the simple Christians had little influence on political and social questions. The absolutist prince felt himself responsible not only for the state, but also for the arrangement of the social order. Moral theologians not infrequently made themselves *personae non gratae* to the civil authority and had innumerable difficulties with civil book censorship if they ventured a clear word against the currents of the time in even these questions. Beyond that, it was then still considered self-evident that the civil rulers had to care for the Christian order of society, even if they did often enough consider it from the standpoint of their own interests.

The situation today is completely changed. Even among the baptized a *purely secular interpretation* of morality and particularly of responsibility in social life widely prevails. Public life is dechristianized in wide areas. The development of the

196

Christian personality and the Christian family is greatly endangered by this. Behind the mass defections from Christianity stands first of all a social mechanism of dechristianization.[10]

A further influential aspect is the change of form of government and of the style of social life. In a democratic society even the simple Christian bears, in a way unknown earlier, responsibility for the forming of public life. He not only decides with the ballot; he also takes part in a new way in the forming of public opinion.

How does contemporary moral theology respond to this changed situation? It attempts to draw out what is true from the network of errors in the blasphemous slogan "Religion is a private affair." Religion is indeed an entirely personal concern for every individual. It is no longer comprehensible to us today that the "princes" were able to determine which religion their subjects must adhere to. A stronger emphasis on the theology of the heart, a more expressive ethic of feeling, the personal adaptation of Christian truth arising from a deep comprehension of the Good News and innermost freedom, show contemporary man that religion is more than a mere social category or "a cultural superstructure built upon social production conditions." This is the one side of the answer, but the other is just as important.

Instructed by the great social encyclicals, including *Mystici corporis Christi* and *Mediator Dei*, which show the social-salvation aspect of Christian life, present-day moral and pastoral theology strives to do more than care more intensely for the "social sphere of duties" of traditional morality. The entire Christian life is especially emphasized as a life in the community of the body of Christ, as the life of solidarity in a community which builds itself upon the altar and from it also receives the commission to a joint effort to Christianize the entire milieu. *The pastoral care of the environment*, which means the task pressing on Christians today to improve their milieu with unified

[10] P. Schmidt-Eglin, *Le mécanisme de la déchristianisation*, Paris, 1952.

197

strength, will certainly represent a main concern for moral theology of the future. Here the flourishing scholarship of pastoral sociology will be able to accomplish a not insignificant service. It will cooperate especially in broadening casuistry, which has until now considered the *individuum* almost exclusively, by a casuistry that is supported by sociology, that is bound more closely to the entire social reality, and by an organic connection of individual pastoral care with such a pastoral theology.[11]

A comprehensive moral and pastoral theology of the environment which brings all provinces of social life into perspective will perhaps be able to free the political responsibility of Christians, until now all too seldom exhibited, from the suspicion that only a "power-hungry" clericalism stands behind the admonitions concerning these matters. In the greater context of the responsibility of Christians for the entire cultural and social life it can be seen organically and convincingly that even politics must subordinate itself to the dominion of God. A sociologically supported moral and pastoral theology of the environment shows further what colossal significance public opinion has, especially in the age of democracy and modern communications media, and how many political decisions are already pre-decided by it. Therefore, moral theology must turn special attention to the formation of public opinion with all its possibilities.

FRAGMENTATION OF LIFE AND THE CHRISTIAN SYNTHESIS

It was not without reason that H. Sedlmayr's book *Verlust der Mitte*[12] led to passionate discussion. By examples of art it shows how through overspecialization and through the decay of Christian universalism the individual areas of life, even art, which is so oriented towards the totality of things, have lost their mean-

[11] This is the concern of the two works of B. Häring, *Ehe in dieser Zeit*, Salzburg, 1964; and *Macht und Ohnmacht der Religion*. See also Schurr, *Seelsorge in einer neuen Welt*, Salzburg, 1959.

[12] Salzburg, 1956.

ing-giving center. In the chaos of the fragmentation of contemporary life, the call for the saving center, for the unity of life, for the vital integrated viewpoint is audible. This is perhaps the most significant demand of this age upon moral theology. In this situation it can under no condition afford merely to compile a long list of duties, commands, and directions. The most pressing concern of moral theology today is a convincing synthesis of the moral life from the perspective of the wealth of the saving mysteries.

It does not suffice for contemporary moral theology to speak somewhere and somehow of how Christ is the redeemer and the Church is the center and goal of all: this truth must clearly permeate all its parts and its entire manner of presentation. *"Instaurare omnia in Christo"* (Eph. 1, 10), to renew all in Christ, must be the concern vitalizing and animating all.

The Salvation Teaching of Collectivism

THE Christian idea of man sees him ultimately as a man of prayer, the worshiper of God, but according to Karl Marx man is at root determined and defined by his work. "In society," he wrote, "producing individuals—and therefore individuals whose production is socially oriented—is the point of departure."[1] That is the way Marx thought that man and society could best be understood. Yet even this Marxist formulation, indeed even the very phenomenon of Marxism, is a unique if frightening proof that man must be seen, as always, as a praying being: either he is consciously a worshiper of the true God, or he is more or less unconsciously "religious" in the service of his "divinity."

It could be countered that the capitalist is obviously a worshiper of the idols of business and devotes himself to his affairs with a quasi-religious ardor, but that is to miss the point: for any profession—artisan, artist, teacher—can be seen in such a way that it, too, has its "idols" and its "religious" ardor. What distinguishes Marxism is that in it there is no longer the perfunctory embellishment of life with "mere" religion. Marx did not wish to waste any of his energy on religion. As a result, nonetheless, religious forces poured themselves out so much the more intensely in his exclusively economically oriented teaching.

[1] *Zur Kritik der politischen Oekonomie,* Stuttgart, 1921, p. xiii.

He escaped much less from religion than did the bourgeoisie that he despised; his hate was nothing more than elementary hate-love. In the very measure that he attempted to explain the course of human existence without religion, indeed by his interpretation of history to dig away the ground from beneath religion forever, he shows how his thinking and feeling has a religion substratum.

Marxism is in its most profound depths a teaching on salvation. In it there is repeated a kind of belief in revelation, the doctrine of original sin and of redemption by the suffering servant of God, faith in the saving solidarity of man and cosmos. And despite his scoffing at the Christian expectation of the world beyond, he proclaims a fulfillment of salvation which lies beyond all the powers of history and all experience.

THE MARXIST BELIEF IN REVELATION

Karl Marx builds upon the position of Auguste Comte, according to which the age of belief in revelation was succeeded by an age of metaphysics, and this in turn by one of pure science. Science is for Marx—and in this he is a child of his times—synonymous with purely positive science (natural science). Sociology, which forms the key to his system, is for him not a science of the spirit, but "social physics." But the manner and way in which Marxism for a century spoke of pure science, that is, of Marxist social doctrine, did not reveal the sober manner of the physicist or the collector of facts, but had assimilated all the *élan* of religious prophetism. Its judgment on the degeneration of bourgeois-capitalistic satiety and hypocrisy is truly prophetic. His interpretation of history shattered, one might say against its will, "the shelter of bourgeois society against the invasion by eternity."[2] The so-called "scientific socialism" attempts to explain the entire

[2] E. Thier, "Marxism," in *Evangelisches Soziallexikon*, Stuttgart, 1954, col. 702.

past and future social development in believing confidence in the newness and absoluteness of its message. "Historical materialism" replaces all the holy books from Genesis to Revelation: "All past history is the history of class warfare" (*The Communist Manifesto*). Class warfare for its part is the necessary result of the dialectical leaps in the development of the means of production and in their effect on production conditions. The "social physicist" Karl Marx not only revealed the ultimate abyss of world history until now; he also knew to proclaim in apocalyptic colors the entire future development up to the revolution of the proletariat and the classless, absolutely contented and fulfilled society at the end.

In this Karl Marx shows not only the customary characteristics of a Jewish prophet zealous for his message, but is venerated even today by his followers more or less uncontradicted as the prophet of an all-illuminating scientific truth. The masses of workers believed in his message ardently for almost a century, although his scientific analyses were in every respect beyond their comprehension and were widely contradicted by later developments.

The canonization of the "prophet" Marx is most clear in the ever more vehement clashes of the epigoni over the authentic exegesis of his writings. Very seldom in a conscious religion have the holy books been so stressed as the works of a Karl Marx. We ourself have seen them standing in innumerable homes in Russia, and, in great contrast to the wretched living standards, always in deluxe editions. Only against the background of a pseudo-revealed religion can the inquisitions against deviations from pure doctrine and its universally binding exegesis by hagiolatrically venerated followers be understood.

The process of destalinization can indeed create difficult crises for those followers of Marx who believe in his revelation naïvely, but it is on the other hand to be understood only if one proceeds from the fact that Marx in his prophetic qualities appears at least as unimpeachable as, for example, Mohammed in Islam. Stalin has been renounced as the valid exegete and executor of binding Marxist doctrine. But the return to Lenin's exegesis does not mean that in the future a supreme authority of faith for world Communism will be renounced. Rather, this validates its claim to have found the pure, and only now mature, and universally obligatory exegesis of Marxism. The intolerance towards deviation in this is certainly more than "dogmatic." The Moscow leadership sees quite correctly that Communism as a fascinating doctrine of faith, as *the* science, threatens to lose its driving force in the great masses if, following the example of Tito, another authority on the exegesis of Marxism were to be found in every land. In this respect, "orthodox" Marxism not only follows the pattern of secular ideologies, but even meets the essential demands of a religious faith.

The Marxist Belief in a Fall into Sin

Marxism in principle denies any ethical motivation for social demands. It believes in an immanent and necessary pattern of social development. And yet it is not merely the Marxist itinerant preacher who hurls angry accusations against the sins of the capitalists and all cultural and religious "concomitant phenomena" of the capitalistic system. Marx himself sometimes delivered a cool scientific analysis, sometimes a prophetic angry denunciation of the *self-alienation of man by private property.* His assertions against religion followed the same pattern: sometimes it was to him a epiphenomenon of a certain stage of socio-economic development, sometimes the epitome of evil and untruthfulness which must be proceeded against with all weapons and in a spirit of moral indignation. The "scientist" once analyzed: "Religious misery is in one way the *expression* of real misery and in another the *protest* against real misery. Religion is the groaning of the oppressed creature, the soul of a heartless world, as it is the spirit of a material milieu";[3] yet he again issued the summons to battle against religion as though it itself were the great sin.

It is not unequivocally clear in the teachings of Marxism whether the establishment of private property is a falling into sin in the real sense or but an inevitable transitional step in the dialectical process of development. As a final puzzle there remains unexplained in the statements and in the general attitude of Marxist teaching whether an evil principle has broken into world history or whether the entire development of private property and exploitation, as the way to the classless society, is in itself something good. Are the exploiters the innocent victims of an inevitable development and the executors of a historical process, or are they abominable sinners? According to the analyses of "scientific socialism," they are the first, while according to the accusing tone even of scientific writings the latter is right.

The Salvation Commission of the Proletariat

Not only the capitalist, but also the proletarian, according to Karl Marx, is himself alienated as a result of private enterprise. Yes, it is on his shoulders that the entire curse and the burden of past social development lies. But Marx is less concerned with the human embitterment of the exploited and unjustly treated proletariat than with the unique mission of the proletariat on the way to the paradisaical, guiltless future. Only in the Judaeo-Christian heritage does the role which Karl Marx assigned the deprived proletariat become comprehensible. Marx spoke to the latent Christian soul of the working class when he painted before its eyes in the most fervent colors the fruitfulness of its suffering, the heightening progressive deterioration within the dialectical process of development as the way to final salvation for the

[3] Quoted from N. Lenin, K. Marx, and F. Engels, *Marxismus*, 2nd expanded German edition, Moscow, 1947, pp. 206f.

entire society. Class hatred itself here received the halo of a redeeming power; for beyond the aggravating of class hatred and class warfare shines the dawn of a redeemed humanity. This "prophecy" of the suffering "servant of God," of the suffering proletariat as the instrument through which the meaning of history unfolds itself dialectically, found a forceful echo. In almost every country the socialist parties which were under the influence of Marx have turned against every social reform because, in firm faith in the Marxist interpretation of history, they looked upon the absolute pauperization of the proletariat as the necessary gate to the classless society of the final period. Thus those men who aspired to a just settlement based on a society ordered to private enterprise actually seemed to them the most dangerous social reactionaries. For this reason, for example, the German Social Democrats (then not yet separated from Communism) in the era of Bismarck voted against all the laws for the amelioration of the situation of the industrial workers. Yet between the two wars representatives of the "religious socialism" proclaimed that to the proletariat "is entrusted the eternal meaning of this our time."[4]

According to Marxist doctrine, the wicked capitalists, whose greediness and insatiability are of course also damned as "sin," are, on the basis of the sociological laws of dialectical development, the executors of a historical commission by their immoderate efforts towards profit, by their accumulation and by their repugnant exploitation of the workers. The more they are slaves to their inclinations, the more they accelerate the historical process. They dig graves for themselves and the entire exploiting society and thus hasten the revolution of the proletariat. The conciliatory elements, on the other hand, and all "utopian" (that means "led by ethical motives") social reformers, seek to delay the historical process which is striving towards its final goal.

[4] F. Karrenberg, "Marxismus als Glaubensersatz," in *Evangelisches Soziallexikon*, col. 704.

They are the saboteurs of world revolution. Acceleration or restraint of the inevitable dialectic process are the only free alternatives according to the Marxist dogma. For just these reasons the counter-revolutionary socialists, workers who long for bourgeois contentment, and everyone who inopportunely seeks to lessen the class struggle have been more and more vigorously persecuted as true capitalists by genuine Marxism.

The Marxist working class proved in a battle which according to the doctrine of Karl Marx at first would bring only greater need and harder suppression, that it was thoroughly responsive to the idea of the redemption of the world and future generations on the basis of its own suffering. In a modified form the Soviet citizen was told he must renounce the immediate gain of socialist advance in order that he might help with his sacrifice in the liberation of the rest of the world from the yoke of capitalism.

MARXIST EXPECTATION OF SALVATION

The believing Marxist does not await a few social reforms which will make life easier for him. He waits for *final salvation.* Classless society as the final (apparently undialectical) phase after all the dialectical leaps of world history is pictured already by Karl Marx and not less by his followers in the brightest colors of the Old Testament expectation of salvation: all enemies and suppressors of humanity are done away with; there is no more hate and no unordered egotism; each man labors joyfully for society and takes no more than is his due from the provisions which stand open to all. The classless society of the final phase knows no more oppressors because there no longer is any private enterprise, private property, or state.

It is well known how Leninism and Stalinism had to use all the arts of exegesis in order to sustain the expectation of salvation in the future and at the same time to explain why, after the revolution of the proletariat, the golden age had not dawned more perceptibly. The way out was sought in the theory that, of course, Communism can succeed in *one* country, and in comparison to the intolerable exploiting society in the rest of the world does give a foretaste of the final condition; nevertheless, true satisfaction and fulfillment can only come about when the class struggle has ceased throughout the world and has given way to a classless society.

One typically nineteenth-century supposition of the Marxist expectation of salvation is the naïve faith in progress, a secularized form of the Christian faith in an absolute meaning and a glorious fulfillment of world history. It is a teleological explanation of the world, which has its true basis legitimately only in the Lord of history, before whom we will jubilantly acknowledge at the end that he made everything good. The Marxist does not see the teleological course of development as so obviously straight as does the liberal bourgeoisie, whose faith in progress, among other things, he surpasses. The development completes itself according to Marx in dialectical leaps, that is, in hard antitheses and confrontations. Progress can be stemmed by "hindering." Yet the more the oppositions are aggravated and the momentary situation permitted to seem almost insufferable, the more certainly a higher level of development is preparing itself. As a genuine apocalyptic, Marx forecasts the final stage of entire historical development even for an unforeseeable future. The time seems to him to have approached in which all the longing of generations will fulfill itself.

JUDGMENT ON SALVATION INDIVIDUALISM

Admitted that Marxism also worked with intrigue and the demonic art of seduction, it was nevertheless able to attain its huge success among the masses of the workers only because it was able to speak to unfulfilled but nevertheless powerful religious

208

longings. A basic fact written in the heart of man by creation and redemption and never exterminable by apostasy, a fact which, moreover, was vital for a thousand years in the West—that is, the solidarity of the salvation of all mankind and the cosmos—was widely suppressed in the past century. A Christianity turned bourgeois concentrated its entire attention almost exclusively on individual spiritual care. Each person sought only to save his own soul without troubling himself much over whether the world was God's or the devil's. Even the proclamation of the Church, within complete basic orthodoxy, was stamped by the spiritual egotism of individuals. Into the resulting vacuum came the message of Karl Marx. The final salvation which he preaches with fervor is a *salvation of entire humanity*. It is prepared for by the common suffering and solidaric battles of an entire class. Its common perseverance works to the salvation of entire society. In his theory of the indispensable and necessary absolute pauperization of the working class, Marx exacted of an entire generation that it be prepared rather to renounce every amelioration of its social situation than to delay the final salvation.

As the first sin Marxism teaches the self-alienation of man by private property and outside exploitation. This all-explanatory "original sin," according to Marx, concerns at the same time the material basis (the "means of production") as well as the social form of production ("conditions of production") and all the resulting expressions of human society. That all corruption stems from its insubordination to a higher world and that consequently even salvation can ultimately renew the face of the earth only from heaven is incomprehensible to historical materialism. But Marxism still knows something of the "groaning of creation and its expectation of redemption": the human race is in solidarity not only with all men, but also with the cosmos. This Christian truth returns in the Marxist teaching according to which humanity cannot enter into the longed for order unless the material and social order is established in production. Marx insists that this order will be assured when humanity has matured to a completely classless society and solidaric collectivity. It is only natural for Marx to believe that in this classless society of the final phase (final salvation), even nature will have lost its unruliness and severity. It will be a pure joy to work and to live in a nature no longer violated by any self-interest.

Marxist salvation solidarity does not have its origin in the "one God and Father of all," in the "one Lord and redeemer Jesus Christ." Its only "God" is humanity productive in society in full cohesion with the productive forces. The inalienable value of the individual in the sight of God is not acknowledged. Marx pushes forward neither towards the true concept of sin nor towards the true basis of human solidarity, because his entire world along with man is at bottom only a "world of trade"; but an afterglow of Christian thinking still shines on in his teaching. It would be inconceivable at least in its passion and its quasi-religious feeling except as an after-effect of the Christian teaching of salvation and corruption history, of the solidarity of men among themselves and with the entire creation.

To the poorly concealed attitude of capitalists worshiping idols in self-seeking business, Marx contrasts an economics of conscious and absolute solidarity. To a religion of "pure inwardness" proving itself powerless in life, he puts the inevitable question of whether religion is not after all essentially concerned with economic structures and social life. To salvation individualism, which wishes to fly to God alone, away from creation and society, he contrasts the solidarity becoming visible precisely in the social and economic area. Modern Catholic sociology of religion and pastoral sociology has accepted the concerns contained in the Marxist heresy as an occasion to call to mind anew the interaction of religion and society, of religion and earthly realities.[5]

[5] See B. Häring, *Macht und Ohnmacht der Religion;* Schurr, *Seelsorge in einer neuen Welt.*

The Otherworldliness of Marxist Salvation

In one respect, Marxism's expectation of salvation in this world stands in harsh contrast to Christian hope. We Christians hope for a salvation that exceeds all concepts, a salvation from God and in God. Marxism is a chiliasm of much more clumsy materialism than its Judaistic and Gnostic predecessors.

Karl Marx believed that he had uncovered by purely scientific means the innermost law of the world and the real motor of all social and historical development: the dialectical movement of thesis, antithesis, and synthesis put into motion by the material substructure. From this he explained the natural necessity of class hatred and class struggle as the driving forces of progress. He derived everything from this dialectic which alone makes history possible, which moves, as much in the substructure as in the social and cultural superstructure, towards sharper and sharper tensions. Still, he proclaimed the vision of a paradise of classless society, the vision of a kingdom of consummated and eternal peace, of unselfishness and universal contentment. Although Marx saw in history that every synthesis on the one hand bore in itself a new thesis and antithesis and must discharge itself, he nevertheless *believed* that in the end there stood the absolutely perfect and *undialectical* synthesis. According to this conclusion, in the end class struggle and class hatred would have given birth to the kingdom of indestructible love.

One sees that here it is pure prophecy of a paradise which will exist in another world which prevails. Here "social physics" gives way to apocalyptic faith.

Christianity proclaims a salvation otherworldly in its essential content. The redeemer is come from heaven and he will appear again on the clouds of heaven to establish the new heaven and the new earth. And yet the salvation promised to Christians is, in the perspective of history, less otherworldly than the paradise

211

of classless society, lying beyond all lacerating dialectic, promised to the Marxists. For we Christians believe that "God is love" and that his creation and the history set in motion by him bears his mark and witnesses to his love. The decisive engine of history is not the hate of the devil but the love of God and the creature touched by his love. The innermost power which holds this world together and sets it in motion is always love, although true love is still ranged in battle with deformed love. The otherworldly powers of perfect heavenly love are now already entered into the course of this history. Even now this love can be experienced. It is poured out into our hearts and celebrates its triumph in the saints. The kingdom of God's love is already present like leaven in the world. A heartless dialectic of the "princes of this world" does not prevail. The genuine fruitful tensions in world history are set in motion by love and find in it their fulfillment.

A comparison of the Christian and the Marxist understanding of history in this respect can and must confirm that *the Marxist expectation of salvation lies essentially more beyond history than does the Christian*. If Marxism is considered as science, then the apex of science is alchemy; for how, out of a world in which Karl Marx can establish essentially nothing but dialectic, class struggle and class hatred, can there arise a condition of fulfilled and perpetual love?

It will be good if we show those blinded by Marxism in their very hour of awakening from disappointment that they have followed a pseudo-religion with high claims on "faith" but with completely inconsistent proclamations of salvation, and not a pure science. Before the twilight of the idols and the destruction of the idols there must come the objective exposure of the idols. But in this we may not forget that the followers of Marxism are to some extent concerned with true, although falsified, Christian concerns. That means especially that these concerns must be given a place in the Christian proclamation; they must be brought to light in Christian life.

212

"Marxism believes, hopes, and forms with a passion. With this it presents a great question and challenge to Christendom: Does it also take its faith, its waiting, and struggle for the kingdom of God so bitterly serious as the Marxist anti-Church takes its affairs?"[6]

[6] P. Althaus, "Religion und Christentum im Urteil des Marxismus," in *Monatsschrift für Pastoraltheologie,* 45, 1956, p. 230.

TIME OF CONVERSION

The Characteristics of Conversion

THE biblical message of conversion does not consist in an abstract human figure confronting a literal law (Judaism) or an ideal of virtue (Stoicism). According to the Bible, two camps, the dominion of God and Satan with his following, confront one another in reality. Two forces struggle for our heart, the old Adamite man and the redeemed man created anew in Christ and through his Spirit. The teaching of conversion gives the answer to the question of how the two camps and the two ways of existing oppose one another in the world and in the heart of every man.

CONVERSION AND THE ULTIMATE EXPERIENCE

Conversion is simply the work of separation, at the end of which Christ, the victor in the great confrontation, will hand over those on the left to the pool of fire and lead those at his right home into his kingdom. We understand the biblical assertions on the incomprehensible change, on the violent revolution which fulfills itself in conversion in the light of the last things, in the light of the judgment that begins on Christ's cross and will be made manifest to all on the last day. It is the passage from death to life, from darkness to light, from lies to truth, from damnation to salvation. It means a rebirth in God (Jn. 1, 11. 13; 3, 35), a birth from above, "in the Spirit" (Jn. 3, 5), adoption by God in a true "new creation": "If any one is in Christ, he is a new creation; the old has passed away, behold, the new has come" (2 Cor. 5, 17).

From the urgent brevity of the saving fullness of the end of time, conversion receives the character of radical decision. On the cross the fearfulness of the final battle (Rev. 8, 20) and the seriousness of God is made visible, in the resurrection of Christ we see his victory: already the outlines of the last judgment and of the final triumph of God are painted before our eyes. Who could wish to settle down complacently between the two camps? Who could play with death when the life of the world has already won its victory?

The end of time is the time of separation and of a holy radicalism. But it is still the interim, a phase between the resurrection and Parousia of the Lord, in which the New which has broken upon us, the divine dominion constantly in process, is still veiled. The fronts of the battle are drawn very clearly, of course, in the cross and in the resurrection of Christ. But the separation of men into the two camps is still in progress. For humanity it will be concluded only with the Parousia, for the individual man with death. *This entire time is under the sign of conversion.* The knowledge of this truth guards the individual and the entire Church from that dangerous triumphalism which was again and again indicted and deplored at the Second Vatican Council and which had formed a largely incredible "style."

The reconciliation of the radicalism of the already begun last age and the veiling of the interim period—the violent upheaval in conversion and its still unfinished character—presents difficult questions. They have found their false expression in the Lutheran expression *"peccator simul et justus."* In this view the "convert" retains in this temporal world essentially the inner form of existence of the "sarxist," Adamite man. His justification, his new form of existence, is reserved for him in the gracious judgment of God; it remains beyond this life. In accordance with an inevitable automatism the old trunk puts forth its bitter fruits; in the same way the fruits of conversion grow in the manner of an automatism—by the power of the irresistible act of the gracious God—out of fiducial belief which is put on from without and which alone merely covers over the conversion.

In Catholic teaching, after the first and basic conversion— after justification—a virulence does indeed still persist from the Old, but the New takes its stand beside it. This battle does not run on one-sidedly between the "wicked world" outside and the angel in one's own breast. These forces struggle with one another in one's own heart as well as in the world. But it is not a battle on the same plane of existence. In the heart of this interim God's dominion has already established itself. Perhaps the devils conquered by Christ in the judgment battle may still pursue their work in this world. But already the Church succeeds in restraining them. How forceful her word and sacrament would be if our culpable failure did not obtrude and retard them! The same holds true of the individual who has been justified: the victorious powers of Christ at the end of time are in him; he is a new creature. If he gives the powers of the age to come (Heb. 6, 5) no place, it is free and genuine guilt, not merely an external addition.

Thus in Catholic teaching conversion is treated with bright optimism, but an optimism which does not permit one to wait idly for the kingdom of God to break in from heaven. The last things are effective signs as much of the hope of the soul converting—for conversion proceeds only from a forceful hope— as of the judgment on the lazy servant.

Conversion and the Kingdom of God

The *eschata* are simply the kingdom of God which some day will be manifest and even now is always beginning, veiled. *The powerful and urgent invitation to conversion proceeds from the coming of the kingdom of God.* "Jesus came into Galilee, preaching the gospel of God, and saying, 'The time is fulfilled, and the kingdom of God is at hand; repent, and believe in the gospel'" (Mk. 1, 14f.). The establishment of the dominion of God in this world by the incarnation, the death, and the resurrection of Christ and by the sending of the Holy Spirit creates for the sinful world the gracious possibility of a return home. The single stipulation is the humble acceptance of this loving dominion in Christ. For this reason Christ's preaching on conversion constantly repeats the demand for the childlikeness which gratefully lets itself be endowed (see Mt. 18, 3; Mk. 10, 15).

Conversion is a grateful and joyous acceptance of the kingdom of God as God wishes to establish it between the day of Pentecost and the Parousia. Therefore, the question of how the kingdom of God is present in the interim is most important for a theology of conversion. If it is an affair of "pure subjectivity," then conversion means a mere change of disposition, to which little or nothing in the affairs of this world matter or can matter, because the kingdom of God would not have yet begun for them.

If the kingdom of God is a power which will come from heaven unexpectedly only at the end of time, then conversion can limit itself to mere fiducial belief and in pure subjectivity give the course of the world over to the devils.

Scripture and tradition make other assertions about the kingdom of God: the Lord himself is "the light of the world" (Jn. 8, 12; 9, 5), so too his kingdom is comparable to a city on the mountain, a light on a stand (Mt. 5:14f.). "The kingdom of heaven is like leaven which a woman took and hid in three measures of meal, till it was all leavened" (Mt. 13, 33). "You are the salt of the earth; but if salt has lost its taste, how shall its saltiness be restored?" (Mt. 5, 13). Thus the acceptance of the kingdom of God and with it also conversion in the strict sense means entering into the intentions of God towards the world and the earthly community. Through the converted, through those who have opened themselves to the dominion of God, the world and the community should feel something of the "first fruits of redemption," of the already proclaimed loving dominion of God (see Rom. 8, 19ff.).

It is true that the turning to the kingdom of God does not happen primarily with a view to the world and earthly affairs, but as a response to the saving invitation and saving works of God. And yet the complete turning of man to the kingdom of God would renew the face of the earth: for one cannot give himself to Christ and his kingdom and then stand indifferent to the great work of his redemption, which is valid for all creation. Though the Christian knows that the final consummation of the world lies in the eschatological future and will be effected by God alone, he is nevertheless also conscious that the future kingdom has already begun with Easter and Pentecost and that the converted have the privileged task of manifesting to all areas of life God's claims to dominion and the saving intentions of the redeemer.[1]

Certainly, conversion in the sense of the gospel is primarily transformation of the heart, the happy turning to a new conviction, a life hidden in Christ. There is no doubt that the "rebirth in God" must show itself first in the disposition, in a new basic relation to God and to one's neighbor and to the good. But conversion is no partial act alongside our life, but an incident of indivisible totality.

As the coming of the loving dominion and of the kingdom of God also means the redemption of the cosmos, of all things—which means the establishment of the saving dominion of God in Christ over everything that is created—so genuine conversion of the individual and of the community always also demands and signifies a change in the milieu.

We are still the world even after we are transplanted into the

---

[1] See B. Häring, *Macht und Ohnmacht der Religion,* pp. 51–67.

kingdom of God. Indeed, the transition from the "wicked world" into the kingdom of the delivering love of God can be accomplished in us only if we let the "first fruits of the blessed freedom of the children of God" come to the world which hungers for redemption—to our own milieu, especially. If I wish to make a genuine and effective conversion, I must at least will to convert myself together with my milieu. I cannot honestly say *yes* to God's dominion in my heart if I do not affirm God's dominion in the sphere of my life with the contribution of my entire heart and all my powers. It is indeed the entire Christ, the saviour of the world, who wishes me to transform completely.

The kingdom of God which has begun in Christ is a *"kingdom of love"* especially concerned with the salvation of all men. Acceptance of the kingdom of God—and that means conversion—is, therefore, a solemn obligation to the law of love and to its vital center, the apostolic zeal for the salvation of one's neighbor. The entrance of God's right of dominion in the world, the fulfillment of the commission to be "leaven and salt of the earth," and the fulfillment of the kingdom's great commandment of love form an inseparable unity. If one hands over the world to the devil and withdraws into pure subjectivity, not only is the recognition of the divine dominion lessened, but the achievement of salvation in the midst of a corrupted environment is made more difficult for a great number of people.[2]

The Church of this interim is not to be equated simply with the kingdom of God, but she is the beginning, the sign, and the instrument of the gracious dominion of God. For this reason she can be called "the quasi-sacrament of the kingdom of God." Conversion thus has an ecclesiastical aspect. Acceptance of the kingdom of God means a *yes* to the Church as the community of salvation in which we are delivered and in which and together with which we may and must act for the salvation of the world and for the honor of God.

[2] See *Lebendige Seelsorge,* 8, 1955, with the over-all theme "Pastoral Care in the Environment."

"The kingdom of God is like a grain of mustard seed" (Lk. 13, 19). The law of growth is suited to the kingdom of God as a whole. The same is therefore also true of conversion. Not only the conversion of the full number of the chosen, but also the complete conversion of the individual is subject to the law of gradual growth. The great break—the transition from the kingdom of darkness and damnation to the light of the life of grace—is customarily prepared amid an entire chain of helping graces. In the same way, the newly given divine life needs a long time to develop itself fully. Usually, only the final *yes* to the loving will of God in death brings final maturity. But one thing must not be overlooked in this: the great transition from death to life with Christ does not proceed from the forces of this world but is a powerful new creation by God. From the human point of view it is a breakthrough, a violent revolution against the old condition; from God's view it is a regeneration, a rebirth in the Holy Spirit. Only God can bestow growth on the "mustard seed" of his kingdom—but not, of course, without the free cooperation of man.

Because we must understand conversion from the perspective of the kingdom of God, it is clear to us that the growth of the new life in individuals must not be isolated from the growth of the kingdom of God as a whole. The salvation of the individual stands in most intimate connection with the fulfillment of salvation of the kingdom of God. Each man opens himself to the growth given from above particularly by praying and working for the coming of the kingdom.

Thus all statements about the relation of the kingdom of God and conversion point to one thing: to the active solidarity with the concerns of the kingdom of God. The summons of the Christian to the apostolate does not stand only as an inevitable addition at the end of his conversion. At all his steps the man becoming and struggling should in gratitude and co-responsibility be conscious of his unity with the concerns of Christ and of immortal souls.

THE GOOD NEWS OF THE RETURN HOME

The Vulgate's translation of Christ's first call to conversion has also contributed in obscuring one essential characteristic of the sermon on conversion. It gives the Greek word μεταγοεῖτε as either *poenitemini* (Mk. 1, 15) or *poenitentiam agite* (Mt. 4, 17). This could give the impression that the sermon on conversion was in essence concerned primarily and perhaps completely with the summons to works of penance. The Greek word in the original text means in its direct philological sense the radical "thinking around." It has, however, still another tone if one knows that the word in the Septuagint was the rendering for *schub,* or returning home. So the sermon of Jesus, preached in Aramaic, was not a direct summons to "penance in sackcloth and ashes," but the good news of the already begun era of the great return home, of renewed hearts, of the kingdom of heaven which has come very close.

In order that the message of the possibility of returning home can be thus correctly accepted as good news, the consciousness of the wretchedness of sin and the need of redemption must, of course, be alive. Only the person who understands the homesick longing of the exiled people can suspect the jubilation which is released by the call of the prophet: The time of homecoming is come. This aspect of the penitential sermons of the prophets and the penitential rites of the old covenant has had such a great significance that the call to conversion can be understood rightly as good news. Papini in an overstated poetic fiction presents a hell growing ever more hellish and devils growing ever more devilish, who finally, having arrived at the extreme abyss of evil and torment, say to themselves: "Our defiance has gone far enough; we must humble ourselves and convert." It doesn't happen that way. Man does not approach conversion through increasing evil, but through growing insight into his sin and into the misery of being cut off from God. Our world today is truly

224

sinful enough to say, "This has gone too far; we must convert!" What is needed today is a serious effort to bring the humanity cut off from God, the open or concealed neopagans, the entire misery and injustice of sin, to consciousness so that the preaching on conversion, preaching on offered salvation, can really be understood and accepted as good news. But the sermon on sin must be very clearly oriented to the good news of the inconceivably glorious coming home to the paternal heart of God, to the unending privilege of being taken into the kingdom of God.

Just what is the idea of penance then? Is it only a concealment of the good news? By no means! Without penance, or at least the readiness to do penance, there is no true lasting and profound conversion. But it is important that the stress not be misplaced. Tediousness must not be placed in the foreground. One must not wish to call in and harvest the "fitting fruits of conversion" (Mt. 3, 8; Lk. 3, 8; Rev. 23, 20) before one has sown the joy over the homecoming. Of course, in further progress the one must be furthered with the other and by the other. So many conversions beginning well do not last because the seriousness of the desire for penance, the sense for expiation in the face of the just God, the *yes* to the cross of Christ was not awakened. But perhaps a still greater number of men have not set out on the way of conversion because it was not proclaimed and exemplified for them as the Easter message.

Not only the first reversal and return to God—culminating in justification, in the rebirth in God—but also the second conversion, the *conversio continua,* stands essentially under the "law of grace" and can therefore be correctly proclaimed only as good news. Certainly, we must always also hear the accusation which the law, especially the chief commandment and the sermon on the mount, raises against us; even our very contrition and humility in view of our past sins must call us to ever deeper contemplation and return, and to penance. But from the Catholic perspective this is not the primary thing. In the foreground of our consciousness and our proclamation must stand the experience of the good news: "He that is mighty has done great things in me!" The call to the intensification of conversion in the New Testament proceeds especially from the *magnalia Dei*: You are consecrated; fulfill this in your life! You are the children of light; therefore walk as children of light! You have risen with Christ; let that be visible in the way you live![3] "He who says he abides in him ought to walk in the same way in which he walked" (1 Jn. 2, 6). He who is converted and constantly called to a more profound return is not subject to a merely exterior regime of law; he is subject to the order of grace (Rom. 6, 14). The life of grace given him and each new grace call him to continuous conversion and to a lasting growth in the good.

SACRAMENTAL STRUCTURE OF CONVERSION

Christ oriented his own sacraments to conversion. The basic sacrament of homecoming is *baptism.* Already in the work of John the Baptist the preaching of conversion formed with the baptism of conversion a unity which was a type of the coming baptism of the Spirit which was to be the actual sealing of conversion.[4] Justin the apologist calls baptism "the bath of conversion which can wash only those who are converted."[5] In the bath of rebirth Christ gives assurance of his gracious meeting to those returning. He makes them like himself and takes them to himself irrevocably.[6]

After baptism, no first conversion, no conversion from death to life, should any longer be necessary. It is a great miracle of God's compassion that he offers to the baptized soul who has again turned from him the sacrament of penance as a second

---

[3] See Rom. 6; 1 Cor. 5, 7ff.; Eph. 2, 1ff., 4, 20ff.; Col. 1, 21ff., 2, 20ff., 3, 1ff.

[4] Mk 1, 4; Lk. 3, 3. 16; Acts 13, 24, 19, 4ff.

[5] *Dialogue with Trypho,* 14, 1.

[6] See Rom. 6; Col. 3, 1ff.; 1 Pet. 2, 22ff.

Easter gift. The remaining sacraments are "sacraments of the living": they are intended to bring the grace and friendship with God already present to maturity and to perfection. For this reason we might also call them sacraments of the second conversion.

All sacraments have the eucharist as their center. This makes clear that the meaning of the second as well as the first conversion is an ever more fervent meeting with Christ.

In the light of the teaching on the sacraments, which are indeed all in some way oriented to conversion, the character of conversion as taking place within the kingdom of God reveals itself still more clearly. "The sacraments designate and effect incorporation into the Church. As signs of the Church the sacraments are gifts of grace within the community and for the benefit of the community; they are appointed to build up and to deepen it."[7] Thus the effective language of the sacraments shows us that conversion is always also a gift from the fullness of grace and the apostolic spirit of the Church and signifies a gracious membership in and obligation towards the Church. The reception of the sacraments will only attain its full fruitfulness, and conversion will only then fully mature, if one tries to become a vital, solidaric-feeling, actively cooperative member of the kingdom of God, the Church.

All the sacraments are cult signs and signify the orientation of our entire life to "worship in spirit and in truth." Baptism, the basic sacrament of conversion, effects the release from sin through "consecration," through the being placed in the glory of God in order to glorify God. As consecration received in baptism is the fruit of Christ's sacrifice on the cross, so the stamp of baptism orients Christians to the valid and heartfelt participation in the glorification of the Father in Christ. The sacrament of re-conversion, the sacrament of penance, restores the cult-worthiness bestowed by the character of baptism and confirmation, or, as the *Pontificale Romanum* says in the rite of penance,

7 *Pastoral Directives of the French Episcopate,* nos. 4 and 11.

it gives the sinner "back to the altar." The radical orientation of the entire life after conversion, and even the conversion itself to the glorification of God, is a powerful imperative of grace: *for those returning home are given their commission not by a mere positive commandment, but by the gracious act of God in Christ and in the Church.*

Sin and Holiness as Social Phenomena

THE fact that holiness has a specifically social radiation, and that there are sins which are palpably social phenomena, is expressed clearly in every moral theology. Obviously, holiness includes care for the salvation of one's neighbor and joint responsibility for the community. In the separation of moral theology into three spheres of duty (duties towards God, duties towards oneself, duties towards one's neighbor) which has become somewhat customary since Kant, duties and sins of the social order are explicitly placed together. Every catechism names sins which offend against the social order or against the salvation of one's neighbor in a special way, such as cooperation in the sins of others, scandal and seduction, slander and divorce, irreverence, disobedience and rebellion. However, the following is not concerned with describing a special area of social undertakings or of offenses against social duties, but with a basic view of holiness and sin as a whole: *holiness and sin are from their very roots and in every manifestation essentially social phenomena.*

SOLIDARITY IN ADAM AND IN CHRIST

The corrupt solidarity in Adam and the saving solidarity in Christ is one of the central themes of St. Paul and, following him, of the Church Fathers. "For as in Adam all die, so also in Christ shall all be made alive" (1 Cor. 15, 22). Death and life, sin and holiness, are essentially related to the fathers of the human race, to the first father Adam and to the new head of redeemed humanity, Christ. All have sinned in Adam. From Adam, through original sin and through the greater and greater accumulation of total guilt of individuals and all communities together, a fearful current of corruption, a staggering unholy solidarity continues to act in human history. No one is able to free himself from this current alone, by his own power. Christ, *consecrated for us* by the Father (Jn. 17, 19), did not break through this ring of corruption by desiring simply to place himself outside of it, outside the history of the first Adam and his descendants. Rather he assumed the full liability of the entire burden of sin. He is the Lamb of God who takes away the sin of the world (Jn. 1, 9). The text does not speak of sins in the plural but of the coalescing corrupting power of sin along with its cosmic aspect. The very emphasis on the lineage of Jesus stresses clearly that he wished to take upon himself the historical burden of Adam. Perhaps the most pointed and daring formulation of this incomprehensible solidarity in which Christ has entered the circle of destructive solidarity in order to burst the chain is given in 2 Corinthians 5, 21: "For our sake he made him to be sin who knew no sin, so that in him we might become the righteousness of God." The force of the sin of human history has been concentrated in the passion and death of the Lord, in his abandonment on the cross; Christ wishes to let himself be struck by it. The force of sin has raised its arm in the battle with the servant of God for a final blow because it senses its true conqueror here. The new solidarity of salvation and holiness has become reality in the most extraordinary solidarity, a solidarity arising from love, of Christ with a humanity enmeshed in corruption: in Christ we have become the righteousness of God. We have entered into the wonderful manner in which God's own

230

justice acts in this corrupt age. In Christ, who consecrated himself for the world, we too are consecrated. For this very reason no one may consider this new life of holiness and justice as his own possession, as it were, for which he alone must care. "And he died for all, that those who live might live no longer for themselves but for him who for their sake died and was raised" (2 Cor. 5, 15). But to live for Christ, according to Paul, means above all to live in solidarity with all members of the body of Christ. Because Christ did not live for love of self, no one consecrated in him may any longer live to please himself (Rom. 15, 1f.). "The law of Christ," as the new law of holiness, means simply "Bear one another's burdens" (Gal. 6, 2). Obviously, this does not refer to the mere patient toleration of the errors of one's neighbor, but to the basic responsibility for the salvation of the neighbor, and then, together with the neighbor, for the salvation of everyone, for the community.

It is especially important to realize clearly that this is not an additional law of a special holiness alongside other laws; it is simply and plainly the law of holiness, of the holiness manifested in Christ, to which we are so wonderfully likened. Our justification and sanctification rest essentially, of their innermost nature, on the saving solidarity in Christ. There is no way leading out of the corrupted solidarity of sinful humanity other than the fundamental saving solidarity of the body of Christ.

Just as the sanctification of Christ means a self-consecration for the world, so there is no Christian holiness apart from entering into this sanctification of one's self, this dedication of one's self by Christ for others.

THE KINGDOM OF CHRIST—THE KINGDOM OF SATAN

The biblical report of the falling of the first parents into sin already emphasizes the involvement of human guilt with the evil of the devil, with the *"non serviam"* of Satan. This aspect of sin comes more and more clearly to the fore in the course of salvation history.

Nothing contributes so much to the scandalizing of a shallow moralism and liberal enlightenment as the many allusions of the gospels to the personal appearance of Satan, to the battle of Jesus with the fallen angelic powers. Whenever the saving power of Christ reaches a peak of its effectiveness the devil, in his most vigorous resistance, becomes aware of his predicament. From the beginning of Jesus' public life to the mystery of his cross this adversary is never absent. The same thing is illustrated for us by the history of the saints, beginning with the legendary embellished temptations of the hermit Anthony and continuing up to the nocturnal attacks of the devil on the holy Curé of Ars. The innermost core of world history cannot be grasped if one deals only with the abstract concept of virtue and of vice. The history of the world and the history of salvation are ultimately the battle between the forces of darkness and the bearer of light—Christ: *"Lux oriens ex alto."*

All "ἀδικία," all blasphemy and all unrighteousness of sin, concentrates itself in the "ἄδικος": in that which has ventured to oppose the holy God to his face; all "ἀνομία," all lawlessness, has as its final instigator the lawless one, the "ἄνομος": him who revolted against the law of holiness. All darkness and lies (σκότος and ψεῦσος) stand in very concrete solid connection with the διάβολος, the confusor who attempts to disguise evil in charity, darkness in bright enlightenment, who defames even Christ himself.

The true disciple of Christ must know in full consciousness that his battle is "not merely against flesh and blood" (against human weakness); behind all temptations which arise from our hearts, but especially behind those which have their origin and seat in the milieu, in the deceitful world "full of lust of the eyes, lust of the flesh and the pomp of life" and again and again address our earthly egotistical way of life, open to the solidarity

232

of corruption, there stand "the principalities, the powers, the world rulers of this present darkness, the spiritual hosts of wickedness in the heavenly places" (Eph. 6, 10ff.).

This battle at the end of time between the two hosts takes place in the atmosphere surrounding us, *in our milieu;* Christ works through the community of salvation; the devil works through the collective, through the *Zeit-Ungeist* surrounding us, which as it were envelops men in the milieu and befogs them when they do not join the communities of salvation and radiate an atmosphere of love, goodness, sincerity, and clear vision around themselves.

In the description of the armor of the Christian soldier in the letter to the Ephesians two basic rules become especially clear: we do not stand alone; our protection and shield are the common faith, the common hope, the love and harmony uniting us with Christ. In this battle no one may believe that he is of himself able to stand firm. Second, we may never persist in mere defensive attitudes, but with Christ we must bear the message of salvation into our environment. "Having shod your feet with the equipment of the gospel of peace, . . . take the sword of the Spirit, which is the word of God" (Eph. 6, 15ff.).

The conquest of the *"sarx,"* which is nothing but our self-glorifying, egocentric way of thinking and manner of existence, coming out of the old solidarity of corruption, is simply not conceivable by merely being concerned for one's own salvation; for the personal forces of destruction—"the principalities, the powers, the world rulers of this present darkness"—constantly make use of the social forces of the milieu, of the atmosphere, to incite the appetites of the *"sarx."* Conscious saving solidarity—and all the assertions of holy Scripture point to this—is the only way to break the chains of destructive solidarity. Anyone who wishes to place himself outside the common struggle falls between the pulverizing strength of the two hosts irreconcilably fighting one another. "He who is not with me is against me, and he who does

233

not gather with me scatters" (Lk. 11, 23). The togetherness, the social way of acting, belongs just as characteristically to holiness as—with reversed omens—to sin.

The deep-rooted determination upon active commitment to the affairs of Christ is an essential part of Christian holiness. It is worlds apart from the zealous but egotistical "striving after virtue" as understood by a liberal, enlightened ethic. Holiness and sin are constantly and from their innermost core the ways of expression of the two eschatological hosts, of the kingdom of God on the one side and the *civitas diaboli* on the other side. This eschatological confrontation takes place in the arena of world history, in the arena of social life.

Christ and his opponent stand opposite one another in full separation, determination, and irreconcilable enmity. The evil one has no share in Christ. But in the social world in which the battle runs its course, even in the Church insofar as she is evident in the milieu, these two so incompatible realms and powers do not yet stand opposite one another in clear separation. *"Perplexae sunt istae duae civitates in hoc saeculo invicemque permixtae, donec ultimo judicio dirimantur."*[1] In the field of this world, of this our human community, the Lord has sown his good seed, but the devil has also sown his weeds. The final separation will take place only on the day of judgment. But in the meanwhile the dreadful battle and even the separation are continually in progress: holiness and sin are incompatible. The two kinds of love, the love of God even to forgetfulness of self and the love of self even to forgetfulness and hate of God, set in motion all the power-formations of world history, the social phenomena no less than the individual events linked with them. In the progress of the eschatological confrontation they crystallize themselves more and more clearly. The purer a man's love is and the more he progresses in holiness, the more clearly he stands in the forefront of the transformation of social life; the more a man hardens

[1] Augustine, *De civitate Dei*, lib. I, cap. 35; see lib. XI, cap. 1.

himself in sin, the more hopelessly is he charmed by Satan as a helper's helper in the collective of evil.

The Social Character of Cultic Holiness

The sanctification and holiness of man mean an orientation towards the glorification of God. A man is holy in the measure that God manifests the splendor of his love to him. The immediate response to the revelation of the splendor and holiness of God is worship, cult. The Church is the *"kabôd Jachwe"* in an even more sublime manner than were the people of the covenant of the Old Testament (Zech. 2, 9; Is. 43, 7).[2] She is the community of those consecrated in Christ. That means that she is the community in which the splendor and holiness of God engrossing her especially shines resplendent and which therefore is capable and obligated to return God the due response of worship, of glory. All sanctification and holiness of the individual is a partaking in the holiness of the Church, of the mystical body of Christ. And so too the response of the individual to the sanctifying action of God is to be understood as participation in the worship of God through the Church.

God desires to glorify himself in this world most especially by forming humanity in Christ to an image of his own unity of love. The command of public worship does not stand somewhere alongside the chief commandment of love of God and neighbor. God wishes to glorify himself before the world precisely through the forming of a community of love by those consecrated by him. The Lord himself explains this to us after the institution of the New Testament sacrifice: "By this my Father is glorified, that you bear much fruit, and so prove to be my disciples" (Jn. 15, 8). The mark of the disciples—in the context this is inexorably clear —is their recognizable, perceptible love and unity visible in social life. Christ as the One consecrated by the Father in the

[2] See also B. Häring, *The Law of Christ*, volume II, pp. 168ff.

Holy Spirit has completed the work of glorification by the most perfect love for men, by the most perfect expression of loving unity and solidarity with us. Sacrifice and sacrament are simultaneous and in one "mystery of holiness" and "mystery of unity and love."

In this view of Christian holiness St. Ignatius of Antioch warns the presbyters that their college should prove itself "worthy of God" by its complete unity of intention and aspiration with its bishop. "This is why in the symphony of your concord and love the praises of Jesus Christ are sung. But you, the rank and file, should also form a choir, so that, joining the symphony by your concord, and by your unity taking your keynote from God, you may with one voice through Jesus Christ sing a song to the Father. Thus he will both listen to you and by reason of your good life recognize in you the melodies of his Son."[3] In this essentially social, proto-Christian view of holiness and divine worship, it is obvious to Ignatius that Christians assemble regularly in order to present, in the most complete expression of community with the bishop and the presbyters, a worthy cult to God the Father in Christ. But only "through love will you form a choir of love and sing a song to the Father."[4]

Sin is separation from the community of those consecrated to the honor of God. In its asocial character itself it is a refusal to adore God. "He who absents himself from the common meeting, by that very fact shows pride and becomes a sectarian."[5] Holiness urges one towards a communal liturgy, but the sinner says, "That is my private affair."

From this essentially social consideration of holiness and sin it also becomes clear among other things how disastrous the results must be if the communal adoration of God, the Sunday "attending of Mass"—even the term betrays itself—is treated as a mere positive commandment.

[3] Ignatius of Antioch, *Ad Ephesios* 4, 1.s.
[4] *Ad Romanos* 2, 2.
[5] *Ad Ephesios* 5, 3.

236

The Freedom of the Children of God and the Dynamic of Satan's Collective

The involvement of moral life with the immediate milieu and the total influences of the social environment, which have been described irrefutably by modern sociology, even by the sociology of religion, have made the defense of a purely individualistic concept of freedom absolutely hopeless. This research has performed a great service for Christian self-understanding. We too are forced by this viewpoint to ponder more deeply the social aspect of holiness, freedom, and sin, and correspondingly to listen more respectfully and more attentively to the pertinent statements from revelation.

In contrast to the individualistic concept of freedom of certain Christians of Corinth and Rome, who in the name of Christian freedom heedlessly ignored the decisive concern for their neighbor, for the effect of their actions in the concrete milieu, Paul presents the true freedom of the children of God, who are free from all self-seeking: "I have made myself a slave to all, that I might win the more. . . . I have become all things to all men, that I might by all means save some" (1 Cor. 9, 19–22). "None of us lives to himself, and none of us dies to himself" (Rom. 14, 7). We partake of the blessed freedom of the children of God in the measure that we feel ourselves fully in solidarity with the salvation of others. The man free in Christ assists in freeing others from the enslaving power of sin and of death. The converse of this truth is: "Every one who commits sin is a slave to sin" (Jn. 8, 34). The first two chapters of the Letter to the Romans delineate the social (asocial) perversions which result from sin. The Lord himself speaks of the power of sin acting as an icy breath upon our own time: "And because wickedness is multiplied, most men's love will grow cold" (Mt. 24, 12). The darkness working in sin, its corruption, the entanglement in guilt and lawlessness—all these different aspects of sin will, if they can once establish themselves in the community, in the en-

237

vironment, exercise there an oppressive, paralyzing effect, narrowing freedom more and more.

In this vision of the "blessed freedom of the children of God" St. Paul sees even out beyond the personal-social sphere. He sees the cosmic dimension. If we let ourselves be led by the Spirit of God and so are truly free (Rom. 8, 14), we confront the longing of creation for the manifestation of the children of God. Creation with her structures co-formed by men, her "state-of-being," groans on the one hand under the slavery to which she is subjected as a result of the sins of men. But she also already lies in labor, she partakes of the first fruits of the freedom of the children of God.

Moral freedom is no fixed quantum. It becomes the responsibility of each individual, but of each individual *as a member of the community*, and also the joint responsibility of the community. All acts which proceed from true freedom—and that always means from true responsibility for the community, too—mean an investment in freedom. All acts of holiness increase the abundance of holiness in the world. Every culpable refusal, every failure to use a genuine possibility of freedom, narrows the scope of the freedom of the person and indirectly also of the community. Therefore, the "πένθος," the "spiritual sorrow" of the Oriental saints and monastic Fathers, has as its particular object the misuse, the nonuse of special graces insofar as such as misuse would be an obstacle to the advent of the fullness of salvation.

The saints can change the environment. Only those who dedicate their entire freedom—and the freedom of the children of God always means the preparedness to sacrifice as well—and their entire love for the "spiritual" forming of the community surrounding them, are on the way to holiness. Not only the extraordinary charismata but every grace is always given in view of the community. The man who does not use it sins against his neighbor, sins against the fullness of holiness of the body of Christ. The theology of saving solidarity exposes the ultimate roots of so many connections within the sociology of religion.

The desertion of the elite is the most disastrous sin. The person who wishes to sanctify only himself, who wishes to leave his neighbor to his fate and the world to the devil, is the furthest removed from holiness in the Christian sense. "If one member (of the Body of Christ) suffers, all suffer together; if one member is honored, all rejoice together" (1 Cor. 12, 26).

The person who thinks legalistically and purely individualistically will perhaps say to himself in the face of great graces, in the face of the possibility of a final breakthrough to a high level of the blessed freedom of the children of God: "There exists no law for all, so I am not obligated; a degree more or less of merit —that is my affair." From the law of holiness, in the light of the mystery of the mystical body of Christ and the *corpus diaboli*, it is crystal clear to us that those who have been favored by God with special graces also bear the greater responsibility.

Great saints have altered the fate of their parishes, their dioceses, and even entire nations. Sociological charts which present the identifiable signs of strength of faith can still chart the paths and spheres of effects of great saints, but they also show the chilled areas around secularized abbeys which still continue after decades and centuries.

Behind the ascertainable sociological dimensions of holiness and of sin, of the freedom of the children of God maturing to the highest perfection, and of the remnant of freedom which for many is gradually approaching the null-point in a tainted milieu, there stand, of course, hidden radiations of hidden holiness and the poison of inner sins working themselves out in secret. A hidden saint in Carmel—even if she does not proclaim her message to the world audibly like St. Therese of the Child Jesus—has perhaps a greater share in the renewal than the most forceful herald of a renewed spirituality and pastoral care. But their charism and their responsibility is given to both for the sake of the community. And we must always be anxious about whether they realize it.

If the renewal directed towards the needs of pastoral care

and especially of liturgy is to be accomplished, then we must remain true to every grace. We need silent, hidden sacrificial souls, worshipers with "faith to move mountains," but ultimately also men who will bring courage, patience, and humility so that, if God hears the sacrificial souls and worshipers and grants them these charisms and tasks, they will be able to work for these great concerns. Where the salvation of God is in progress, where God consecrates someone to his work, the saving solidarity will be perceptible in a special way; that community of the saints which is the representation of the great community of salvation will be formed in an experiential and visible manner. To this the victory over destructive solidarity is promised.

New Currents in Catholic Spirituality

THE great elaboration of the primitive Christian idea of the mystical body of Christ by such theologians as Emile Mersch, and the unique echo that this primitive Catholic message found in the entire world, demonstrate clearly that our time has been prepared in a special manner for the proclamation and the incorporation of this truth of the saving solidarity of all in Christ. And though the impulses to this new solidarity are derived from primitive Christian teaching, and are faithful to the gospel and to the constantly proclaimed truth of the Church, the fact that they have so spontaneously come to bear anew in various lands and social classes while the same truths and motives a hundred years ago found only a very modest response, is also doubtlessly connected to the altered social structure and the corresponding different sort of experience men have.

The large economic organizations and modern mass society cannot of themselves awaken a genuine Christian spirit of community. But always where men take the gospel and the law of grace seriously, there grows in the face of new conditions, of new ways of experience, of new spiritual possibilities and dangers, that Christian answer which seizes the day as profoundly as possible in order to sanctify it, and so to overcome most effectively what is dangerous within it.

EXTENSION OF THE FIELD OF VISION

In this age of internationalism the countless economic and cultural contacts of the peoples and continents heighten in Catholics the feeling of a universal belonging-together in an entirely new way. Where others speak of chance community, Catholics experience the solidarity of the peoples as the unity of the family of God. The various Catholic world congresses with their extraordinary participation of the laity bring home more strongly than in earlier times the experience of abundance in variations and reciprocal responsibility.

A new springtime of world mission, above all a clearly perceptible readiness to sacrifice on the part of youth, can be seen in almost all Catholic countries. Now also the laity go out with the missionaries in ever greater numbers as mission doctors, technicians, nurses, and the like. European and North American dioceses place more and more priests at the disposal of the dioceses of Latin America which are short of priests. Thus, to name only one example, the archbishop of Munich, who himself had no superfluity of priests, gave several South American bishops the permission to solicit among his diocesan priests. The priests who declared themselves ready to work in South American dioceses received their full salary from the archdiocese for five years, for those dioceses are also financially poor. Similar things can be reported from many other countries. Truly unique are the actions of the National Catholic Welfare Conference of America, which stands ready to assist the needs of all countries.

World-wide solidarity and at the same time appreciation of distinct groups is fitting for a genuine Catholic spirit. But if the danger of individualism, which scoffs at revelation and the entire historical development, and likewise the danger of unthinking compliance to the pull of the mass culture are to be resisted effectively, then the many worthwhile tendencies in the direction of a genuine spirit of community must be consciously developed.

242

Anyone working in this direction is certainly doing it primarily and ultimately out of loyalty to the mandate of the Lord and in reliance upon his grace; he can nevertheless also do it with the special confidence that he is responding to the *kairós*, the command of the historical hour. In this he can count on the valuable, vitally powerful psychical experiences of modern man. Because the solidarity of all peoples is already more and more strongly perceptible in the natural area of the economic and political, the good news of the unity of God's family and the saving power of the love which unites all can embody itself so much the more easily.

Business and Technical Science

The distorted prominence of the reward-motif in some Catholic circles, indeed even in the ascetical literature of the past centuries, is doubtless to be seen in good part as a reflex of the "mercantile society." It was because the relation to neighbor and to community was considered one-sidedly from the standpoint of the barterer that the genuinely biblical basic idea of reward and punishment could suffer noticeable disarrangement and distortion and finally assume an excessively broad place in the thought and motivation of many. Not infrequently, the "reward of a child" of which the Bible speaks—the reward which is completely one with the love of God which gives of itself and which blesses—was subtly infiltrated by and confused with the reward haggled over in the market.

The modern working world is no longer determined primarily by merchants—despite the monstrous importance of the modern advertisement whose effect on the intellectual life should be expressly studied—but by the unanticipated technical art of production. Not the *homo mercator* but the *homo faber* is the ruling image in today's business. The mere motive of reward can no longer speak to modern man so immoderately and one-sidedly. Already because of the prevailing mode of experience it finds its correct place more easily. Man of the technological, atomic, space age stands meanwhile in temptation of supposing that everything, even the relation to God, can be planned out and produced. If he remains religious despite a way of thinking formed by the technological way of life, then a new danger, Pelagianism, can become exceptionally acute; man believes he is able to order his relation to God of himself and with his own strength. If he is not as successful in perfecting and modeling himself as he is with material stuff, then he despairs and devotes himself exclusively to the technical sphere. Catholic spirituality can nevertheless also seize upon the good in this modern kind of experience: man is more than a merely mechanical performer of an abstract law; he has himself received from God the gift of recognizing his powers with all their special possibilities and of fulfilling the goals of each. The believing man is able to grasp the *kairós*, the constantly new offer of the hour, and with the help of the grace of God to fulfill its mandate. Man is a historically powerful being, able to form the progress of history so much the more powerfully the greater his loyalty to the special grace and the special possibilities and needs of the community is. The modern Catholic thinks less of the reward than of the correct relevant form of his action, of the divinely willed success of his work and of the joy of being in the right place.

A New Serious Appreciation of Earthly Realities

Because of the unique fragmentation of modern society and the joint democratic responsibility for its formation, the amazing abundance of technical-scientific information and the fascination with even more astounding inventions are no longer able to separate their religious life from their profane life. As a result in the past decades there spontaneously arose on every side a call for a theology of earthly realities.

If modern science and technology in their first flush attempted to some extent to escape the grasp of religion and set themselves up in a somewhat inimical fashion as purely profane reality in opposition to the immediately religious, there can be seen today among the religious elite and simultaneously among the influential representatives of science a clear turning away from a secular, profane view of earthly realities. With unique consciousness they walk in the bright light of the dogmas of creation and redemption. It is recognized that salvation history does not simply pass by outside the history of technology which has become so exciting and full of suspense for modern men, nor alongside the laws of sociology and psychology which are studied with the joy of discovery. If Christians take up the situational possibilities, a new *universitas scientiarum* from a religious perspective, a regaining of the religious center, can result.

Connected with these efforts towards a more developed theology of earthly realities is also the promising growth of a positive spirituality of marriage and family. Today no well-instructed preacher would any longer dare say in front of well-instructed Catholic laity, "One can save his soul despite marriage and family." The young Catholic elite of today knows very clearly that just this high evaluation of virginity also forms an essential presupposition for the appreciation of marriage as a vocation in the full sense and in conscious fulfillment of God's holy order to sanctify in marriage the spouse, one's self and the children, and thus to glorify God.

REFLEX ATTITUDE OF CONSCIOUSNESS

A reflex attitude of consciousness towards the decisive areas of human existence suits the modern type of man who plans and forms in a technological way. While the rural man throughout the millenniums had a relation to objects and especially to life which was formed by his observation of spontaneous growth and maturation, modern man, because of the altered economic foundation, lives much more reflectively. In the vital area of life, in marriage, he also begins to calculate much more consciously and to plan reflectively. The strength of the Catholic spirit shows itself precisely in the correct mastery of such new attitudes of consciousness. The Catholic elite of today need not emphasize in a crotchety manner that one accepts life in marriage just as it comes. The elite can give a much more pertinent answer to the arrogant kind of *homo faber* to whom the procreation of new life is little more than sober calculation of utility, if it fundamentally bases itself on the ground of the new attitude of consciousness, but implements it in a Christian way. The Catholic family that is strong in faith says *yes* even today to an abundance of children, not fatalistically or with dull resignation, but in a completely conscious, reflexive responsibility, in an attitude of conscious grateful preparedness to respond to the gift bestowed by God. Whereas the mere *homo faber* reckons the number of children with regard to this world, with regard to his standard of living, to his comfort and social standing, the Catholic elite asks: "How do we recognize the will of God in the natural gifts of temperament bestowed on us, in our power of faith, in our physical and psychological health and finally also in our economic means?" That is not sober calculation, but conscious listening to the call of God. So the modern Catholic in married and family life is able to attain a much higher level of reflective, alert consciousness than his merely economic, utilitarian planning contemporaries; and yet in this consciousness he does not in any way lose his sense of security in God's economy nor the confident affirmation of the task of creation.

This example is typical of many other areas. The modern open-minded and well-educated Catholic is psychically formed to a high degree by the structures of modern business and modern mass society; but the decisive formation which distinguishes his way of life and his thought about the world from that of his unbelieving neighbor is received from the world of faith.

It is true that the Catholic elite of today must become still much more clearly conscious that, seen as a whole, it will be impossible for it to master all the powers of formation which are present in the contemporary economy and society if it does not consciously work at providing the economics and society of today with healthier structures. We still are not, for example, sufficiently clear that especially the mass means of propagating opinion (the press, films, radio, television) in the age of democracy and collective forms of life are powerful positive possibilities for us, that they require a more conscious asceticism and an articulated art to place them in closer cooperation with all good things in the service of truth. It would already be a great blessing if the decree of Vatican Council II on the means of communication (*De instrumentis communicationis*) could awaken the proper attention to the high significance of this truly new world and sharpen the conscience in this area.

How Shall the Foolish Become Wise?

AT the time of the novena of Pentecost, when we pray with the apostles for the fullness of the gifts of the Spirit, Peter, the prince of the apostles, warns us: "Be wise!" How shall we become prudent? The liturgy gives us the answer.

Of ourselves we are fools, imprudent. We remain so as long as we trust in ourselves. We become wise only when we await everything from the gracious power of God. "For we ourselves were once foolish, disobedient, led astray, . . . but when the goodness and loving kindness of God our Saviour appeared, he saved us, not because of deeds done by us in righteousness, but in virtue of his own mercy, by the washing of regeneration and renewal in the Holy Spirit, which he poured out upon us richly through Jesus Christ our Saviour" (Tit. 3, 3-6). It is the grace of God which "trains us to renounce irreligion and worldly passions, and to live sober, upright, and godly lives in this world" (Tit. 2, 12). Only the unmerited grace of God can make us wise. But grace is not at man's disposal; he cannot even merit it. In order to become wise, he can do nothing better than pray. "Be wise and watchful in prayer" (epistle). Only the man of prayer who opens himself to the wisdom coming from God is able to become wise. The unwise, earthly minded man believes himself wise when he forges his own plans; the Christian may and must know that he is wise and prudent in the measure that he remains docile to the providence and gracious guidance of God. As men of the *eschaton*, of the time of pentecostal fullness, we gather together with Mary and the apostles for persevering prayer. Only the man who is watchful and listens to what God says to us can be a true man of prayer. But in the long run one can be watchful and perceive the loving intentions of God in all things only if he preserves unceasingly the attitude of the man of prayer who awaits all things from God's goodness.

Earthly prudence always asks what is to be gained for the self. The man of prayer, however, who is wise in intercourse with God, sees his greatest chance in demonstrating love for another. Therefore, the apostle himself explains his understanding of the true wisdom of the watchful man of prayer in this way: "Above all, love one another, for charity covers a multitude of sins." The self-centered person is always finding a hair in his soup. In intercourse with others he sees first of all the unfavorable, the divisive. He believes that first of all with the scales of a kind of balancing justice one must measure out punishment or censure to the other and reward and merit to oneself, before one may engage in the venture of love. Genuine Christian wisdom will never come to this venture in such a way. On the contrary, bold love, love according to the manner of Christ, first covers the errors of others with the mantle of love— and has confidence in the risk of love. Is this not the new way of confronting the brothers and sisters who like us confess their membership in Christ, although they are not yet united with us in the Church? The unwise man thinks he must first dispute, settle the historical account, and only then think of a dispassionate expression of love. He is on a wrong track which cannot possibly lead to unity. The wise men who in prayer are touched by the spirit of Christ take the burden of others on themselves, and so release themselves on both sides from historical guilt and obduracy. Thus they open the way to a loving recognition of truth.

Men with shopkeepers' souls, who appear prudent, always ask what one is obliged to do—under pain of sin or even under pain of serious sin. But Christian prudence, which bestows "the Spirit of truth," looks at the received gift of grace and asks how it can best be used for the neighbor and the community. The Christian does not thus dwell on a "purely supernatural plane." The natural and the supernatural form a single order. The man who looks at earthly goods as the exercise ground of egotism does not open himself to the supernatural gifts of grace. For this reason Peter warns in one breath: "Be hospitable to one another without murmuring!" and "Serve one another, each with the gift of grace which he has received, as good stewards of the manifold grace of God!"

The man who is wise in the manner of Christ is not concerned first of all nor exclusively with bringing his own ship into port— "Save your soul and let the world go to the devil." He knows that all our salvation and deliverance fulfills itself in the service of brotherly love, and in the manner in which the Spirit prompts each to act. "If someone speaks, then let him speak God's word; if someone performs a service, let him do it in the strength bestowed by God, so that in all things God may be glorified through Jesus Christ our Lord."

The gospel completes the image of the wisdom of the Christian which must appear to the world as foolishness, but which bears all blessedness in itself, for it comes from the "Comforter," whom the Lord sent us from the Father. Filled by the Spirit of truth, we see in the magnificence of the Easter splendor the "folly of the cross," the blessedness of the testimony of love. "You will bear witness to me" is the proof of a confident love even in the midst of misunderstandings and persecutions.

The collision of "the folly of the cross" with the prudence of this world is unavoidable. We sense that within ourselves. Does not the "old man in us" secretly scoff at every valiant start towards Christ-formed wisdom which we attempt? We must not take scandal if even within the Church the truly wise are now and then looked at askance, or even at an occasional attempt to exclude the saints "from the synagogue," because they dare to have a more courageous understanding of the law of Christ than the teachers of the law who cling too much to the letter. The Lord has predicted that to us. But we will successfully conquer the temptation in our hearts and the attack from without only if the Lord himself purifies us through the baptism of fire of the Holy Spirit and makes us strong in holy joy and gratitude. "Filled with holy gifts, we ask you, O Lord, grant that we may at all times remain giving thanks" (postcommunion prayer). The Holy Spirit is the gift in person. He is bestowed. He teaches us to look upon all in the conferring will of God. He teaches us to gain everything in loss, to find in the surrender of our self the true self in God. Only the Spirit of Christ can teach us courageously to affirm the sacrificial love of Christ as the true law of our lives.